The Mystical Circle of Life

You Are Immortal

isbn 0-9710116-4-8

The Mystical Circle of Life

You Are Immortal

Robert Elias Najemy

**May the pain of loss be lightened
as the light of truth shines in our hearts.**

TABLE OF CONTENTS

Note: The following chapters were originally included in this book, and are considered important for your understanding of the subject. As they are now, however, included in the book Universal Philosophy, you may read them in there

INTRODUCTION

This book is an announcement of joy and freedom – an affirmation that we are immortal spirits, powerful beings, who have been fooled into mistakenly thinking that we are small, fragile, limited, incapable and mortal. It is only our beliefs that limit us. This book is based on logical thought patterns which help us to bridge the gap between reason and faith.

Because of a personal need to understand more about death (after encountering the death of loved ones and friends) I was moved to make an intensive research into what was known about death. My search led me through the investigation of various religions, philosophies and psychological studies on dying patients, as well as on those who have been clinically declared dead and have come back to life.

It has also led me to do my own research on the subconscious contents of a large number of people through special relaxation techniques and hypnotic regressions. My search also led me to investigate some of the more sophisticated, and in my opinion, reliable communications from spirits on the other side of the veil which separates life from death.

I found the **same truths to be repeated** over and over again by these various sources. Everywhere I looked, the same facts seemed to be reaffirmed. It became obvious that death was not the end of anything but the physical body. The rest of the being was simply changing its level of focus, like changing the channel of a TV– a new reality is tuned in to. The real *being* does not stop existing, it just sheds its material covering. I became convinced by the sheer agreement of so many sources.

Then, when I realized how many people fear, cry and suffer needlessly because of their impending death or because of the death of a loved one, I felt the need to share this information with whomever is ready to receive it. There is so much unnecessary misery in the world which is caused by a lack of knowledge of the reality of life. I hope that this book will help in some way.

In this book we cover many aspects of the relationship between life and death. We start with an investigation into what happens after death according to these various sources. Then we examine how we may live our lives so fully in harmony that we are always ready to leave the physical body peacefully and with dignity, whenever that time might come. This analysis helps us to discover if, in fact, we are living our lives to our greatest potential and in harmony with our real values.

Then we look into how we may help those who are dying around us to approach this culmination of their physical life with peace and dignity.

We then discuss the possibility of reincarnation, i.e. whether the soul might have the possibility to create a new physical body and return to this earthly plane for further spiritual development. In the examination of this possibility, we investigate the various scientifically documented cases of past life memory.

In the last chapters we are presented with some useful philosophical concepts which help us to understand the relationship between the body, mind and spirit as well as between the spirit, God and nature.

(**Note:** As the custom is to refer to the third person singular with the male pronoun, we will for convenience do so, but in each case we equally mean he or she, him or her.)

I hope that this book will be useful to you in your search for greater inner peace, harmony and self knowledge.

THE BENEFITS OF FACING
AND ACCEPTING DEATH

We have so much to gain by studying and overcoming our fears of death. By doing so:

1. We are thus facing the truth of the mortality of our physical bodies rather than hiding from the only sure thing in life – death.

2. We in this way become more **spiritually mature and aware.**

3. We become **more fearless** as most of our fears are related to death or to the loss of what we are attached to.

4. We are **freed from the need to compromise** our **values,** beliefs or life purpose, such as in the examples of Christ, Socrates, Ghandi and Martin Luther King who, because they never feared death, never compromised their values.

5. We are allowed to **look consciously at our relationships.**

6. We are directed to **look consciously** at our behavior and **conscience.**

7. We are **freed** from a **superficial life,** allowing us to live a life with meaning.

8. We are allowed to **put love above** any other factors.

9. Everything is put into perspective – the spiritual, mental, emotional, and– material.

10. We are able to **prepare and be ready for the transition** whether it be ours or our loved ones with less pain and anxiety.

11. We are more **capable of helping others** when they are close to their death or the death of their loved ones.

CHAPTER I

WHAT HAPPENS AFTER DEATH?

(A study of 12 well respected sources)

A) FACING LIFE AND DEATH

You and I are going to die some day and so are all the people we know. It may be soon or it may be in 60 years; the fact is that we will some day have to leave these physical bodies.

Birth and death are the only events which all human beings have in common. What happens between birth and death will differ from one person and the other, but all of us are born and all of us will die. In spite of the fact that we all have this common destiny, we seldom discuss it or squarely face the fact that these physical bodies are mortal and temporary.

We live in a«death denying society», in which people simply ignore the reality that these bodies will soon once again be dust. When the end does come close, we are left unprepared, shocked, angry, depressed, confused and in general, unable to cope with the situation.

According to Pascal, «People being unable to cure death, try not to think of it». The purpose of this book is to help the reader face death whether it be close at hand, or far in the future; whether it be his own death, or the death of a loved one; whether it be a sudden death, or a long drawn-out illness.

Preparing for death means preparing for life. A person who is able to face death is able to face life without fear or attachment. Facing death is a great emotional, mental and spiritual exercise that helps us gather our inner forces, leaving us more capable of facing life here and now. Our look into the various aspects of death **will not be a morbid preoccupation with something negative** but rather an intelligent investigation into what exactly happens when we leave our physical bodies. We are not running away from life but rather, lifting up our heads and opening our eyes in order to look squarely into the eyes of life which, of course, includes death. It need not be an unpleasant subject to investigate or discuss.

Almost all of the information which we have about death is that it is most likely one of the most pleasant experiences of our lives. The overwhelming consensus of all the religions and most of the philosophies of the world is that **life does continue** after death, that life exists before and after life in the physical body.

Imagine a radio which is playing music. The life of the radio is the electricity which is passing through it. When the radio wears out or breaks down it plays no more music; it is no longer alive to us. But the life of the radio is the electricity which existed before the radio was created and after its destruction.

In the same way we are the life which exists before the creation of the physical body and after its return to the state of dust. In this investigation we shall take a look at what some of the various religions, philosophies and scientific surveys have to offer us concerning this question of, «What happens after death?».

The sources of the information which we used are as follows:

<u>RELIGIONS:</u>
Christianity
Hinduism
Tibetan Buddhism
Islam

PHILOSOPHIES:
Socrates - Plato
Theosophy

COMMUNICATION FROM THE SPIRIT WORLD:
Seth (who speaks through the personality of Jane Roberts in America)
Alice Bailey (who writes communications from the masters without physical bodies).

SCIENTIFIC SURVEYS:
Dr. Raymond Moody's investigation of over 150 people who have died and returned to life.
Dr. Osis' study on the experiences of over 1300 cases of dying patients in hospitals in the U.S.A. and in India.
Dr. Elizabeth Kubler-Ross' research on over 1000 dying patients in hospitals in the U.S.A.

HYPNOTIC REGRESSIONS:
Psychiatrist Helen Wambach's research on over 750 hypnotic subjects concerning their experiences before birth and after death.

Our purpose will be to examine the similarities and differences between these various widely differing sources. It seems logical that if so many differing sources give similar information, then there is a greater likelihood that that information is valid and true. Let us address ourselves to the first question which comes to our mind – «Do we continue to exist after death?»

B) IS THERE LIFE AFTER DEATH?

The world famous psychiatrist Carl Jung points out that all religions believe in existence of life after the death of the physical body.

«Each of the four religions affirms that there is a subtle and death-surviving element - vital and physical - in the physical body of flesh and blood, whether it be a permanent entity or Self, such as the Brahmic Atma, the Moslem Ruh, and the Christian Soul, or

*whether it be only a complex of activities (or Skandha) psychical
and physical, with life as their function (the Buddhist concept).
Thus, to none of these faiths is death an absolute ending, but to all
it is only the separation of the PSYCHE from the gross body».*

Sri Satya Sai Baba, who teaches that all religions lead equally to the
one God, affirms that at death we simply remove these bodies as if
removing clothing.

*«Death is a state very much like sleep. The individual discards this
body like an old worn-out suit of clothes. Only the body perishes.
As the mind has no physical form, it does not perish with the body,
and thought activity persists even after the death of the physical
body».*

The great ancient Greek philosopher Socrates believed the same. In
Plato's *The Last Days of Socrates*, more specifically the *Phaedon*,
Socrates gives numerous arguments, explanations and logical
reasonings convincing those around him that life must certainly
continue after death and furthermore, that in that bodiless state,
the soul has even greater potential for **self-knowledge**. (This last
point concerning the opportunity of self-knowledge at the point of
death is corroborated by the Tibetan Book of the Dead).

Greek Orthodox Theologian G.V. Meletis in his recent book *What
Happens After Death* praises Socrates' unwavering faith in the
soul's immortality.

*«But the most incomparable example of faith in the immortality of
the soul in history, is that of Socrates. In Plato's «Phaedon», his
genius mind uses unrivaled dialectics to support and prove his
faith in immortality. He defines death as a mere separation of the
soul (from the body), a fact which is not unpleasant at all, but
rather, it is a release from the limitations of the body, which its
senses, enslaves the soul. The soul and body, according to
Socrates, are related to each other in the same way as the guitarist
and the guitar. The body is the guitar and the soul is the guitarist.
Death, which destroys the guitar, does not in any way harm the
guitarist.»*

Truly, it would be **difficult** to find an enlightened thinker in history who did not believe in the existence of the soul after death.

Alice Bailey wrote dozens of books through the process of automatic writing in which she was guided by souls who had shed their physical bodies and were trying to help mankind by communicating the truths that they saw from their higher viewpoint. She explains that the movement from life to death is simply a shift of consciousness from one plane of existence to another; something like the transfer of consciousness from waking, to dreaming to the deep sleep state. It is a change of focus.

«Death is essentially a matter of consciousness. We are conscious one moment on the physical plane and a moment later we have withdrawn onto another plane and are actively conscious there. Just as long as our consciousness is identified with the form aspect, death will hold for us its ancient terror. Just as soon as we know ourselves to be souls, and find that we are capable of focusing our consciousness or sense of awareness in any form or any plane at will, or in any direction within the form of God, we shall no longer know death».

Many psychological surveys have been recently conducted in which patients, who have been declared clinically dead, and then returned to life, were questioned about their experiences. The most famous of these are the research studies of Dr. Raymond Moody and the psychiatrist Elizabeth Kubler-Ross. Dr. Moody's research is published in his book *Life After Life*, in which he analyzes and exposes many common experiences, among these, who have died and returned to life.

Elizabeth Kubler-Ross's findings are published in her Books *On Death and Dying*, *Questions and Answers on Death and Dying*, and *Death - The Final Stage of Growth.*

In other studies, Dr. Osis found amazing similarities in the experiences of over 1300 dying patients in hospitals in India with those in the U.S.A. Dying patients were questioned about their experiences such as having visions of lights, visitations by deceased relatives, or hearing special sounds.

Doctors Moody, Osis and Kubler-Ross have all come to a firm conviction concerning the existence of the soul after death. Dr. Kubler-Ross has boldly announced to public audiences that concerning her belief in life after death that *«It is not a matter of belief or opinion. I know beyond a shadow of doubt»*. She has spoken equally conclusively about her belief in reincarnation.

Another psychiatrist, Helen Wambach, made hypnotic regressions on over 750 subjects, bringing them into the memory of the experience of their prebirth existence. Both she and her subjects were quite bewildered by their experiences in the hypnotic trance; all now have a firm conviction in life **both before and after** life in the physical body. Her research makes interesting reading in her book entitled *Life Before Life*.

Thus we have a unanimous **YES** from all our various sources concerning the question: «**Do We Exist After Death?**»

C) WHAT HAPPENS AT THE POINT OF DEATH?

As we try to examine the point of death, it seems to be as elusive as the point of falling asleep. What exactly happens at the point of falling asleep? At which point can we divide the sleep state from the waking state? Obviously there is no actual point of falling asleep – it is a gradual and imperceptible process. "Seth" explains that the process of dying is very similar.

«What happens at the point of death? The question is much more easily asked than answered. Basically, there is not any particular **point** *of death in those terms, even in the case of a sudden accident».*

Seth is a spirit who has supposedly finished his evolution on the earth plane and is communicating through the mind of Jane Roberts in the U.S.A. Many extremely interesting books have been communicated through Jane by Seth; *The Seth Material*, *Seth Speaks*, *The Nature of Personal Reality* and others. Seth explains that death is an integral part of the growth process. He points out that if we did not go through numerous psychological deaths we would never mature and manifest our inner potential.

«Pretend for a moment that you are a child, and I am trying to undertake the particular chore of explaining to you what your most developed, adult self will be like - and in my explanation, I say that this adult self is to some extent already a part of you, an outgrowth or projection of what you are. And the child says, «But what will happen to me? Must I die to become this other self? I do not want to change. How can I ever be this adult self when it is not what I am now, without dying as what I am?»

«I am in somewhat the same position when I try to explain to you the nature of this inner self, for while you can become aware of it in dreams, you cannot truly appreciate its maturity or abilities; yet they are yours in the same way that the man's abilities belonged to the child».

Seth explains:

«As mentioned earlier, all through your lifetime, portions of that body die, and the body that you have now does not contain one particle of physical matter that «it» had, say ten years ago. Your body is completely different now, then, than it was ten years ago. Yet obviously you do not feel that you are dead, and you are quite able to read this book with the eyes that are composed of completely new matter. The pupils, the «identical» pupils that you have now, did not exist ten years ago, and yet there seems to be no great gap in your vision».

We may infer that life cannot continue in the physical body unless these millions of partial deaths take place. There is the illusion of continuity though in reality, the body is never older than ten years old. This is a biological fact. We see the same truth in a forest which seems to be the same forest for thousands of years, but the trees making up the forest are dying and being born every year. The forest seems to be the same but in reality it is different.

Sitting on the banks of a river we see a seemingly constant reality. That river which we were watching a few minutes before is now hundreds of meters downstream. In the same way life is a continuous process. The physical body comes and goes, is born and dies; but the life principle continues unchanged. The evolution of the whole is dependent upon the continual creation and destruction of the parts.

There is, of course, a point at which the spirit realizes that it is out of the physical form and begins to experience life outside of the physical body. Dr. Raymond Moody has constructed a «sample death experience» based on the common factors which he observed in the subjects of his research study who had died and returned to life (in the same body). This sample death experience contains only those elements that were found to be common in the majority of cases and not isolated experiences which may have been found in only a few cases.

«A man is dying, and as he reaches the point of greatest physical distress, he hears himself pronounced dead by his doctor. He begins to hear an uncomfortable noise, a loud ringing or buzzing, and at the same time feels himself moving very rapidly through a long tunnel. After this, he suddenly finds himself outside of his own physical body, but still in the immediate physical environment, and he sees his own body from a distance, as though he is a spectator. He watches the resuscitation attempt from this unusual vantage point and is in a state of emotional upheaval.

«After a while, he collects himself and becomes more accustomed to his odd condition. He notices
that he still has a «body» but one of a very different nature and with very different powers from the physical body he has left behind. Soon other things begin to happen. Others come to meet and to help him. He glimpses the spirits of relatives and friends who have already died, and a loving, warm spirit of a kind he has never encountered before - a being of light - appears before him.

This being asks him a question non-verbally, to make him evaluate his life and helps him along by showing him a panoramic instantaneous playback of the major events of his life. At some point he finds himself approaching some sort of barrier or border, apparently representing the limit between earthly life and the next life. Yet, he finds that he must go back to the earth, that the time for his death has not yet come. At this point he resists, for by now he is taken up with his experiences in the afterlife and does not want to return. He is overwhelmed by intense feelings of joy, love, and peace. Despite his attitude, though, he somehow reunites with his physical body and lives.

«Later he tries to tell others, but he has trouble doing so. In the first place, he can find no human words adequate to describe these unearthly episodes. He also finds that others scoff, so he stops telling other people. Still, the experience affects his life profoundly, especially his views about death and its relationship to life».

Let us examine the various stages of this experience, step-by-step, analyzing simultaneously what our other sources say about these experiences. The first stage is a feeling of struggle between the forces of the body and the spirit at the moment when the spirit is getting ready to leave. This is expressed in the example as reaching the «point of greatest psychological distress». He then feels as if going through a long tunnel from one dimension to another experiencing sounds and lights. These sounds and lights are frequently referred to in the *Tibetan Book of the Dead*, which describes the various after death experiences.

This process in which the "energy–body" and mind separate from the physical body is described in this way by Alice Bailey:

1) The bioenergy, life force, or "prana" begins to withdraw from the various extremities and organs of the body and concentrates itself in the spinal column. This affects the functioning of the nervous, endocrine and circulatory system weakening the body's hold on life. There is a relaxation, a letting go, a release from pain in the body; and the will for life gives in to the desire to now be free from the physical vehicle.

2) The energy then gathers into the seven energy centers located

along the spinal column. There is very little sign of life in the body
at this stage.

3) Then all the energy accumulates into one of the seven centers
depending on the individual's state of evolution. The energy body
and mental body will then exit from that particular center where the
energy has gathered.
a) The average individual who lives basically to satisfy his physical
and personality needs will leave from the solar plexus area.
b) The individual who has learned to share, to love, and to serve
others and is devoted to God, will leave from the heart area.
c) The individual who has gained the higher wisdom of his soul's
nature, and does not identify with the body or mind, will leave from
the forehead center.
d) The individual, who has broken through the illusion of this
physical reality and has recognized his or her oneness with God,
will become enlightened and leave from the center at the top of the
head.

4) According to Alice Bailey, even though the vital energy and mind
have left the physical body there is still the possibility for them to
return as, for example, in the case of Dr. Moody's subjects or in the
resurrection of Lazarus by Jesus the Christ (and of course, Jesus
Himself).

5) When the «soul-mind complex» realizes that it is out of the
body, it begins to experience its new "subtle" or "spiritual body."
This new spiritual body in yogic terms is made up of the emotional-
mental body – the higher intellect and the causal body. These are
bodies made of subtle thought essences which are material but so
subtle that we are not ordinary able to perceive them.

D) THE SPIRITUAL BODY

Here is an account of how one of Dr. Moody's subjects experienced
his non-physical body.

«I pulled on out into the intersection and as I did I heard my friend
yell at the top of his voice. When I looked a saw a blinding light, the

headlights of a car that was speeding towards us. I (heard) this awful sound - the side of the car being crushed in - and there was just an instant during which I seemed to be going through a dark and enclosed space. It was very quick. Then I was fort of floating about five feet above the street, about five yards away from the car, and I saw my friend get out of the car, obviously in shock. I could see my own body in the wreckage among all those people, and could see them trying to get it out. My legs were all twisted and there was blood all over the place. *People were walking up from all directions to get to the wreck. I could see them and I was in the middle of a very narrow walkway. Anyway, as they came by, they would not seem to notice me. They would just (keep) walking with their eyes straight ahead. As they came real close, I would try to turn around to get out of their way, but they would just walk **through** me»*.

We can understand from this man's description that he thought his body was physical in nature until he tried to communicate with people and they «walked right through him». Seth explains that:

«You will find yourself in another form, an image that will appear physical to you to a large degree, as long as you do not try to manipulate within the physical system within it. Then the differences between it and the physical body will become obvious».

According to the *Tibetan Book of the Dead* (written about 1000 years ago) the spirit in its spiritual body can see and hear the happenings in this physical world but cannot be seen or heard (except perhaps in the case of very sensitive people here on the earth who have the ability to hear the messages of these disembodied spirits).

Some of Dr. Moody's subjects verified that they saw disincarnated spirits futilely trying to communicate with embodied spirits. Dr. Moody asked if one of the subjects could see any of the disincarnated spirits trying to communicate with spirits living in physical bodies.

Subject: «Uh, huh. You could see them trying to make contact, but no one would realize that they were around; people would just ignore them...They were trying to communicate, yet there was no way they could break through. People seemed to be completely unaware of them».

Dr. Moody: «Could you tell anything they were trying to say?»

Subject: «One seemed to be a woman who was trying so hard to reach through to children and to an older woman in the house. I wondered if in some way this was the mother of the children, and maybe the daughter of the older woman in the house, and she was trying to break through to them. This seemed to me to be meaning that she was trying to reach the children and they continued to play and pay no attention, and the older person seemed to be going about in the kitchen doing work with no awareness that this person was around».

Seth explains to us in more detail about the powers and abilities of this subtle body. He compares this state to the state of consciousness we experience in our dreams:

«This form will seem physical. It will not be seen by those still in the physical body, however, generally speaking. It can do anything that you do now in your dreams. Therefore it flies, goes through solid objects, and is moved directly by your will, taking you, say from one location to another as you may think of these locations».

«If you wonder what Aunt Sally is doing in, say, Poughkeepsie, New York, then you will find yourself there. However, you cannot **as a rule** *manipulate physical objects. You cannot pick up a lamp or throw a dish. This body is yours instantly, but it is not the only form that you will have. For that matter, this image is not a new one. It is intertwined with your physical body now, but you do not perceive it. Following death, it will be the only body you are aware of* **for some time.**

«Much later and on many levels you will finally learn to take many forms, as you choose, consciously. In one manner of speaking you do this now, you see, translating your psychological

experience - your thoughts and emotions - quite literally but unconsciously into physical objects. You may find that when you imagine yourself as a child - after death - that you suddenly have the form of the child that you were. For a certain period of time, therefore, you can manipulate this form so that it takes any appearance that it had when it was connected with your physical form in the immediately previous physical life. You may die at eighty and after death think of the youth and vitality that you had at twenty, and find then that your form changes to correspond with this inner image.

«Most individuals after death choose a maturer image that usually corresponds to the peak physical abilities, regardless of the age when the physical peak was reached. Others choose instead to take the form they had at the particular point when the greatest mental or emotional heights were achieved, regardless of the beauty or age that characterized the form. Do you follow me?»

The fact that the spirit finds itself in a subtle body after leaving the gross physical body is common to all of the reference sources used for this text. They all seem to agree that it can continue to see and hear what is occurring on the earth level for a period of time, but as a general rule it cannot be seen or heard on the physical level by us who are still limited by physical bodies.

Some spirits who have a great attachment to the physical body and have never thought of themselves as spirits, or have never made the distinction between themselves and their physical bodies, may be quite shocked when they see their physical form dead in front of them, and may even try to reenter it. Of course they will be unable to do so. Seth comments on this:

«It is not common. But nevertheless, under various circumstances, such individuals will attempt to reactivate the physical mechanism, becoming more panic-stricken when they discover the body's condition. Some, for example, have wept over the corpse long after the mourners have left, not realizing that they themselves are completely whole where, for example, the body may have been ill or the organs beyond repair».

These unfortunate souls are, of course, a very small minority of the less developed human beings. Eventually they will overcome their ignorance and continue on their way.

Let us sum up the qualities of this new subtle body that we find our selves in after death:

1) It can pass through objects, and objects can pass through it.

2) It can see, but cannot be seen.

3) It can hear, but cannot be heard.

4) It can move instantaneously from one point to another without the passage of time.

5) The form, like our dream form, is mutable and will change shape and form according to the contents of our mind.

6) As a rule it cannot manipulate physical objects or seriously affect the physical worlds in which we incarnated spirits live.

E) OTHERS COME TO MEET AND HELP US

In the next stage of the death experience we are met by other spirits who come to help us with the transition. These beings are described in different ways by the different sources. Socrates calls them guardian spirits; Seth calls them guides. The various religions call them angels or devas. Moody's subjects had the experience of being met either by relatives or by a being of light who helped them to understand what was happening. The studies of Doctors Kubler-Ross and Osis in the USA have shown that a great number of dying patients have contact with these helpful spirits even **before** they die.

Dr. Osis recorded over 1300 cases of dying patients who had clear visions of spirits coming to «aid the patients' transition into the post-mortem existence». In order to check whether this phenomenon was conditioned by cultural or religious programming, he made the same study in India where he found the same results.

His studies further showed that these experiences were inhibited and not increased by the use of the various narcotic drugs given to the patients to calm their pain. The experiences were not the affect of drugs.

These visions, furthermore, were experienced in the waking state, with the eyes open, and not in the dream state or with the eyes closed.

According to Dr. Osis, «The roots of this type of experience seem to go beyond factors such as type of illness and beyond educational levels and denominational differences».

The same type of phenomenon was experienced by Christians, Hindus, Moslems and Jews alike. One last interesting point that came out of Dr. Osis's study was that some dying people saw the spirits of relatives or friends who, as far as they knew, were still alive. In reality they had passed away but the patient had not been informed for one reason or another. This tends to eliminate the possibility that the patient's logic is entering into the experience, since he or she is seeing the spirit of a relative believed to be still alive.

However, according to Seth it may actually be possible for some of us embodied spirits to help dying spirits in their transition process. This takes place in our dream state.

«As mentioned earlier, however, in the sleep state you may help recently dead persons (or) complete strangers to acclimate to after-death conditions, even though this knowledge is not available to you in the morning. So others, strangers, may communicate with you when you are sleeping and even guide you through various periods of your life. It is not a simple matter to explain life conditions as you know them, so it is extremely difficult to discuss the complexities of which you are not aware. The main point I want to make in this chapter is that you are already familiar with all conditions you will meet after death, and you can become consciously aware of these to some extent».

Thus, while sleeping we may leave our physical bodies and help spirits recently released from their bodies adjust to their new out of body conditions. This presupposes a certain degree of spiritual advancement and experience on our part that enables us to help others. We may even counsel spirits who are about to be born in the near future.

This last possibility is suggested in the results of psychiatrist Helen Wambach's studies on over 750 hypnotic subjects. They were taken back in their soul memory to the point before birth and asked if anyone was helping or guiding them in making the choice about being born (i.e. when, where, to whom and with a male or female body). The results were that:

1) 81% found that they chose to be born.

2) Almost all of these felt they had some guidance.

59% experienced more than one counselor.

And quite surprisingly,

3) 10% had counselors who were already incarnated in a physical body at the time of their birth.

Dr. Wambach's comments:

«*It was interesting to me that 10 percent of the subjects reported people in their current lifetime counseling them before birth. Some would have a mother or father counseling, some would have relatives who had died prior to their birth, some would have people they would know later in the coming lifetime. Oddly, there seemed to be no distinction between people who were alive at the time the birth was being decided upon and people who were dead or not yet born. In the world between lifetimes, our chronological time system and whether one is physically alive or dead seem of relatively little importance*».

Thus a spirit is always alive and able to communicate with other spirits whether it be in or out of the physical body. While locked in the walls of the physical body, our awareness is severely limited to the physical world. But in the dream state we may actually play the role of guide to spirits leaving or entering the physical world.

Greek orthodox Theologian G.V. Meletis in his book *What Happens After Death* affirms that the living do in fact have an "energy body," "astral body" or "spiritual body," however you may want to call it, which is independent of the physical body and can travel in our dreams.

«According to St. Athanasios, the soul is self-supporting and self-moving. It moves the body but is not moved by any other external force. So, since the soul is self-moving, it can also move on its own after separating from the body. «It is not the soul which dies, but the body (that) dies when the soul departs».

«Even when the soul is embodied it isn't restrained. Instead, often while the body is asleep, the ever-wakeful soul leaves the physical body. And although being an embodied soul, it travels to celestial and angelic worlds. It is obvious that the soul can obtain a more clear awareness of immortality when it is liberated from the body. Since it was able to live a bodiless life while being connected to the body, its life will certainly continue after the body's death. The soul is immortal and that is why it thinks and contemplates on immortality».

Socrates believed that at the point of death each spirit is allotted a «guardian spirit». This guardian spirit guides the newly released spirit to a certain place where it must stand trial and account for its actions, selfish and unselfish, here on the earth. Socrates maintains that guidance through these states (which he represents as various rivers and valleys with different qualities) is absolutely necessary, for there are many dangers of losing one's way and becoming confused or lost.

Theologian G.V. Meletis again affirms that Christianity, too, agrees on the need for a guide in the after death states:

«The soul doesn't depart for the life beyond all alone. This is not possible, because even when we go from one town to another we need a guide. Thus, of course a guide is much more necessary when our soul leaves the body and goes to the afterlife».

From the same Christian tradition we have the teachings of Saint Antonios who lived in the Egyptian desert as a wandering monk and occasionally went into trance, had mystical experiences and communications with angels. The text from which this passage was taken is considered to be written around 360 years after the birth of

Jesus the Christ.

«Then, the saint prostrated before the angel and said:

«Thank you my Lord, for you have sent me a guide to reveal to me hidden secrets that I always wished to know».
The angel said to him, «So, go on, ask me» and the saint, replying, said: «In that eternal world, is it possible for dead people to recognize each other?»

«Then, the angel answered: «Look at this world. People go to sleep at night, but when day breaks, they meet each other, greet, talk like friends and act according to prementioned agreements and conversations. Likewise in that other world, people recognize each other and talk; and one can also ask someone unknown to him who he is, just like here. But this is possible only for the righteous ones, and not for the sinners».

«Then the saint asked, «Please tell me also what happens when the soul leaves the body. What is the reason to make requiems and what is their use for the dead?».

«And the angel replied: «Holy Father: when the soul leaves the body, it is taken by the angels to heaven to worship our Lord, Jesus the Christ. But between heaven and earth there are demonic orders which examine the soul. They bring ledgers with them in which every human sin is listed, and start reporting to the angels every sin this person has fallen into.

«For example, on that day of that month he stole; the other day he prostituted; on the other he committed adultery; on the other he masturbated; in that place he lied; and so on.

«The angels also bring their ledgers, in which every good action of the dead is written, like charity, selfless service, fasting, prayer, or other virtues.

«If the virtues of the dead exceed the sins, the angels grasp the soul and lift it to the second level. There they find other demonic orders,

grinding their teeth like wild beasts, insulting the soul and (trying) to snatch it away from the angel's hands. And a great deal of talking and noise is needed for the angels to release this soul from the demon's hands.

«And if they succeed, the soul is raised to the third level and there it finds another demonic order, stronger and wilder... and a big struggle takes place, with so much confusion and agitation, as the angels attempt to save this pitiful soul from the hands of the infamous demons.

«If the soul is delivered it raises up to the next level, and goes on until it reaches the seventh; where there is another demonic order called the «prostitutes order», and no one can describe, Holy Father, the tremendous agitation and noise they make, how they threaten that suffering soul. If the soul was a monk before, the noise is much more loud, and the demons start telling the soul «Where are you going, you, who prostituted and befoulded the angelic form? Go back to the dark and dirty Hell!»

«No language can describe the punishment this convicted soul suffers from the demons! Honorable Father, though I am an angel I feel terrified. Can you imagine the unbearable pain this soul suffers from this punishment?

«But in case the soul is found to be pure of sins, the angels take it and it is blissfully elevated to Christ. Then it sees the angels' dances, the holy apostles brilliance and it hears the angels' melody and enjoys the immeasurable beauty.»

From the angel's explanation to St. Antonios, we can see that following process ensues:

1) The spirit leaves the physical body and finds itself in the subtle body.

2) It is met by angels who take it to the Christ.

3) The spirit then passes through a remembrance of his past actions sinful (selfish) and good (unselfish).

4) This process of examination is represented by the passing through of seven levels of angels and demons who represent the good and evil psychological tendencies of the individual.

If we can wade through all the demons, fear and suffering projected in this text, we can see that it is very similar to the other descriptions of being met by a guide and passing through an examination.

The similarities between this explanation and that given in the *Tibetan Book of the Dead* are amazing. In the Tibetan explanation the spirit passes through seven levels of «peaceful deities» (angels) and seven levels of «wrathful deities» (demons). Before this process of passing through the deities, the spirit is confronted with the Radiant Pure Light (the Christ). Even the timing of these events is similar as will be seen further on.

The main difference, however, between the Tibetan and the Christian explanations is that in the Tibetan text it is explained that all these visions of angels, demons and lights, sounds and fearful and pleasant experiences are simply the **projection of the contents of the mind.**

It is interesting and pacifying that Dr. Moody's subjects felt nothing but **love and understanding** from the beings of light who helped them with their examination of their lives. There was no criticism, judgment or guilt. Could God be anything but love? Perhaps it is time to stop **fearing** God and start **loving** Him.

F) WE EXAMINE THE WAY IN
WHICH WE HAVE LIVED OUR LIVES

Thus we can see that the first function these guides perform is to help us with an examination of how we have lived our lives. We may imagine that life is a school and at the point of death we take our final exams in order to see what we have learned and what we have failed to learn in this life. Seth explains that although after death experiences are subjective and varied, this process of self-examination is one that cannot be avoided.

«Now you may or may not be greeted by friends or relatives immediately following death. This is a personal matter, as always. Overall, you may be far more interested in people that you have known in the past lives than those close to you in the present one, for example.

«Your true feelings toward relatives who are also dead will be known to you and them. There is no hypocrisy. You do not pretend to love a parent who did little to earn your respect or love. Telepathy operates without distortion in this after death period, so you must deal with the true relationships that exist between yourself and all relatives who await you.

«...Then there is a period of self-examination, a rendering of accounts, so to speak, in which they are able to view their entire performance, their abilities and weak points and to decide whether or not they will return to physical existence.

«Any given individual may experience any of these stages, you see; **except for the self-examination,** *many may be sidestepped entirely».*

This concept of a judgment of one's way of life is common to all religions and to all the sources that we are considering in this study.

According to Islam we judge ourselves.

«And every man's fate have we fastened about his neck; and on the day of Resurrection will we bring forthwith to him a book which shall be offered to him wide open: «Read thy book: there needeth none but yourself to make out an account against yourself this day». (Koran 17:14)

In the Christian Bible we are told that we will be judged in the way that we judge others. According to St. Antonios to whom we referred earlier, this examination period takes place from the third to the ninth day after the departure from the physical body. Then the spirit goes to a level of existence in accordance with his behavior, and waits for the final Judgment Day. It seems, however, that the timing of this after death event is extremely variable according to the individual and that, in reality, we cannot even talk about time and space on that level. Time and space appear to be phenomena of the physical world only.

Many of Dr. Moody's subjects had the experience of this «review» of their lives in the short time that they were in the death state. They were able to examine their entire life span in a few minutes or perhaps even instantaneously. Here are a few case examples:

«I first was out of my body, above the building, and I could see my body lying there. Then I became aware of the light-just-light-being all around me. Then it seemed there was a display all around me, and everything in my life just went by for review, you might say. I was really very, very ashamed of a lot of the things that I experienced because it seemed that I had a different knowledge, that the light was showing me what was wrong, what I did wrong. And it was very real.

«It seemed like this flashback, or memory, or whatever was directed primarily at ascertaining the extent of my life. It was like there was a judgment being made and then, all of a sudden, the light became dimmer, and there was a conversation, not in words, but in thoughts. When I would see something, when I would experience a past event, it was like I was seeing it through eyes with (I guess you would say) omnipotent knowledge, guiding me, and helping me to see.

*«That's the part that has stuck with me, because it showed me not only what I had done but **even how, what I had done, had affected other people.** And it wasn't like I was looking at a movie projector because I could **feel** these things; there was feeling, and particularly since I was with this knowledge... I found out that not even thoughts are lost... Every thought was there... Your thoughts are not lost...».*
This is an extremely interesting point that this man makes. He felt exactly how the others felt as a result of his actions. How perfectly

this expresses the law of Karma; that we shall experience some day from others what they have experienced from us.

This also may be the psychological basis of the idea of a *hell*, where the individual experiences the unpleasant effect of his selfishness on others. Perhaps we create our own heaven and hell according to our feelings of peace or conflict with our selves because of our way of life; especially when we see our way of life more clearly after removing the blinders of the physical body and senses.

Here is another case from the Moody files:

«When the light appeared, the first thing he said to me was, «What do you have to show me that you 've done with your life?» or something to this effect. And that's when these flashbacks started. I thought, «Gee, what is going on», because, all of a sudden I was back early in my childhood. And from then on it was like I was walking from the time of my very early life, on through each year of my life, right up to the present».
(And here this girl gave many accounts of the memories that came to her).

She continues:«Now, I didn't actually see the light as I was going through the flashbacks; He disappeared as soon as he asked what I had done, and the flashbacks started... and yet I know that he was there with me the whole time, that he carried me back through the flashbacks, because I felt his presence, and because he made comments here and there. He was trying to show me something in each one of the flashbacks. It's not like he was trying to see what I had done - he knew already - but he was picking out these certain flashbacks of my life and putting them in front of me so that I would have to recall them.

*«All through this he kept stressing the importance of **love**. The places where he showed it best involved my sister; I have always been very close to my sister. He showed me some instances where I had been selfish to her, but then just as many times where I had really shown love to her, and shared with her. He pointed out to me that I should try to **do things for other people**, to try my*

best. *There **wasn't any accusation** in any of this though. When he came across many times when I had been selfish, his attitude was only that I had been learning from them also.*

«He seemed very interested in things concerning knowledge too. He kept pointing out things that had to do with learning, and he did say that I was going to continue learning, and he said that even when he comes back for me (because by this time he had told me that I was going back) that there will always be a quest for knowledge. He said that it is a continuous process, so I got the feeling that it goes on after death. I think that he was trying to teach me as we went through those flashbacks».

How assuring is this description of the examination. There is no judgment, no guilt, but rather an objective observation of what was learned, and what was not yet learned, and a clarification of where we can learn to love more and understand more. Life is a school for learning to love and understand ourselves and others. Seth explains that this examination is necessary before we can move on to higher levels of consciousness after death.

«You examine the fabric of the existence you have left, and you learn to understand how your experiences were the result of your own thoughts and emotions and how these affected others. Until this examination is through, you are not yet aware of the larger portions of your own identity. When you realize the significance and meaning of the life you have just left, then you are ready for conscious knowledge of your other existences».

Seth insinuates here that we have lived other lives and that when we have finished with our examination of our present life, then we may begin to examine and experience the qualities of our previous lives.

«They may, for example, become aware of their own reincarnational selves, recognizing quite readily personalities they knew in other lives, if these personalities are not otherwise engaged. They may literally now hallucinate, or they may «re-live» certain portions of past lives if they choose. Then there is a period of self-examination, a rendering of accounts so-to-speak, in

which they are able to view their entire performance, their abilities and weak points and to decide whether or not they will return to physical existence.

«Any given individual may experience any of these stages, you see; except for the self-examination, many may be sidestepped entirely. Since the emotions are so important, it is of great benefit if friends are awaiting for you. In many instances, however, these friends have progressed to other stages of activity, and often a guide will take the guise of a friend for a while, so that you will feel more confident».

Some interesting ideas are expressed in this explanation by Seth:

1) After completing the investigation of our recently lived personality we then enter into awareness of ourselves as a complex of many other personalities which we have been in other lives.

2) We may even have contact with spirits who played parts with us (i.e. friends or relatives) in those previous existences.

3) We may then evaluate our performance as a whole over the span of the many lives that we have lived. We may mentally relive some of those experiences of past lives in the way we did in the examination of our recently ended incarnation.

4) Then we decide whether we have finished with our lessons on the earth or whether we need to return to earth for more lessons in the school of life.

5) The forms of friends which meet and help us with the transition may be projections of the spirits who actually played those roles with us here on earth, or parts played by guides, who may take the forms of our deceased friends or relatives in order to make us feel more at ease and open to their help and guidance.

The fact that we also examine the actions of other previous lives has been confirmed by an American businessman Walter Cowan who died and was brought back to life some days later by Sri Satya Sai

Baba in India. When Walter Cowan came back to life he gave us the
following descriptions of what he experienced while dead:
*«While in the Connemara Hotel in Madras, two days after I
arrived, I was taken very sick with pneumonia. As I gasped for
breath, suddenly all the body struggle was over and I died. I found
myself very calm, in a state of wonderful bliss; and the Lord, Sai
Baba, was by my side.*

*«Even though my body lay on the bed dead, my mind kept
working throughout the entire period of time until Baba brought
me back. There was no anxiety or fear, but a tremendous sense of
well-being, for I had lost all fear of death.*

*«Then Baba took me to a very large hall where there were
hundreds of people milling around. This was the hall where the
records of all of my previous lives were kept. Baba and I stood
before the Court of Justice. The person in charge knew Baba very
well, and he asked for the records of all my lives, He was very kind
and I had the feeling that whatever was decided would be the best
for my soul.*

*«The records were brought into the hall – armloads of scrolls, all
of which seemed to be in different languages. As they were read,
Baba interpreted them. In the beginning they told of countries that
have not existed for thousands of years, and I could not recall
them. When they reached the time of King David, the reading of
my lives became more exciting. I could hardly believe how great I
apparently was in each life that followed.*

*«As the reading of my lives continued, it seemed that what really
counted were my motives and character, as I had stood for
outstanding peaceful, spiritual and political activity. I do not
remember all the names, but I am included in almost all of the
history books of the world from the beginning of time. As I
incarnated in the different countries, I carried out my mission -
which was peace and spirituality.*

*«After about two hours, they finished reading the scrolls, and the
Lord Sai Baba said that I had not completed the work that I was*

born to do and asked the judge that I be turned over to him to complete my mission of spreading the truth. He requested that my soul be returned to my body, under his grace. The judge said «So be it».

«The case was dismissed and I left with Baba to return to my body. I hesitated to leave this wonderful bliss. I looked at my body and though that it would be like stepping into a cesspool to return to it, but I knew that it was best to complete my mission so that I could eventually merge with the Lord Sai Baba. So I stepped back into my body... and that very instant it started all over again - trying to get my breath, being as sick as you could be and still be alive. I opened my eyes and looked at my wife and said: «You sure look beautiful in pink...».

Afterwards, Sai Baba was asked if Walter's experience was real or some sort of hallucination. Sai Baba replied, *«The experience was a real experience, not an illusion. It was an experience occurring within thoughts».* Then Sai Baba was asked whether every person who dies has similar experiences. Baba answered, *«It is not necessarily so, some may have similar experiences, some not».*

This may be confusing to us that the subjective mental reality is both individually unique and real at the same time. If we think more deeply about the subject, however, we will realize that the same is true of this physical reality, even though the external reality of objects «appears» to be rather stable.

When we leave the confines of the physical vehicle, the mind has even more freedom to create the reality it chooses. This is obviously so in dreams where reality is extremely mutable and created by our thoughts. It appears that the after-death state is very similar. This does not mean that it is any less «real» than the reality that we know here on the earth. Ultimately both realities of physical life and metaphysical life are equally **real** and at the same time equally **non-real,** because they are both temporary and changing experiences without any permanent true basis.

Thus, each of us will have different after-death experiences according to our beliefs and the contents of our minds, but this reality which we create is no less real than that reality we create now here on this earth through our beliefs and mental states.

This is easy to see when observing the different ways in which we react to the same event. One single event in the external world can create hundreds of different reactions ranging from ecstasy to indifference to depression depending on the belief system and programming of the individual.

Can we say that the internal reality of these individuals is not real to them? But none of their realities is real in the sense of being absolute. The ultimate unchanging Reality is beyond both life and death.

Seth explains that our beliefs about life and death and good and evil greatly affect our after death experiences:

«A time of judgment is a useful framework in many instances, for while there is no punishment meted out in your terms, the individual is then prepared for some kind of spiritual examination and evaluation.

«Those who understand thoroughly that reality is self-created will have least difficulty. Those who have learned to understand and operate in the mechanics of the dream state will have great advantage. A belief in demons is highly disadvantageous after death, as it is during physical existence. A systematized theology of opposites is also detrimental. If you believe, for example, that good must be balanced by evil, then you bind yourself into a system of reality that is highly limiting, and that contains within it the seeds of great torment.

«In such a system, even good becomes suspect, because an equal evil is seen to follow it».

W.Y. Evans-Wentz, in his commentaries on the *Tibetan Book of the Dead*, agrees with Seth that these after death states are a function of the contents of the mind of the individual:

«It is not necessary to suppose that all the dead in the

Intermediate State experience the same phenomena, any more than all the living do in the human world, or in dreams.

«The deceased human being becomes the sole spectator of a marvelous panorama of hallucinatory visions; each seed of thought in his consciousness... **karmically** *revives; and he, like a wonder-struck child watching moving pictures cast upon a screen, looks on unaware, unless previously an adept in yoga, of the non-reality of what he sees dawn and set.*

«At first, the happy and glorious visions born of the seeds of the impulses and aspirations of the higher or divine nature awe the uninitiated; then, as they merge into the visions born of the corresponding mental elements of the lower or animal nature, they terrify him and he wishes to flee from them; but, alas, as the text explains, they are inseparable from himself and to whatsoever place he may wish to flee they will follow him».

Thus the visions we will have after death will depend on the way we have lived our lives, and on the way we have treated those around us. Christian Theologian Meletis to whom we have previously referred, affirms that the after death experiences are mental states.

«St. Gregorios of Nissa explains, «Do not think of Hades as a place, but rather as a state of bodiless life, without any precise form».

St. John of Damascus characterizes it as a «mental place». Precisely because the bodiless soul «is formless and therefore is not encased in the body but rather it is contained in the intellect».

«As soon as the soul leaves the body it enters into the so-called Intermediate State. This is the period preceding the rising of the dead and the Final Judgment. During this period the soul preexperiences the good and evil according to its way of living and ending its Life on earth».

According to the *Tibetan Book of the Dead*, we watch the inner battle between the conflicting forces of love and selfishness, good and evil, evolution and stagnation, and the divine and the sensual within us. This is presented as the passing through the visions of the «peaceful and wrathful deities» who are manifestations of our positive and negative characteristics, i.e. love, understanding, compassion, jealousy, fear and other human emotions.

The *Tibetan Book of the Dead* is written to help us guide those who have just left their bodies as they pass through these experiences. We read or speak to the recently released spirits explaining to them the nature of what they are seeing, while explaining to them that everything that they see is, in reality, a **projection of their own mental content.**

«Be not awed. Know it to be the embodiment of your own intellect». We explain to the spirit that these visions are *«thought forms issuing from one's own intellectual faculties».*

We are further told that any prayers, mantras, meditations or spiritual studies which the spirit has made in its life will be extremely helpful to it now. They will give the spirit:

1) More pleasant experiences in the after-death state.

2) The clarity to realize that it is watching the projections of its own mind and not some objective reality.

3) Less fear as a result.

4) The ability to control its mind and merge it with the pure light, with its chosen form, or name of God. We can, through our constant practice of repeating the name of the Christ, direct our mind towards Christ and merge with Him. This presupposes however, a great deal of previous practice in disciplining the mind.

Mr. Evans-Wentz explains these after death experiences more in-depth in his commentary on the *Tibetan Book of the Dead*:

«The apparitional visions seen by the deceased in the Intermediate State (after death) are not visions of reality, but nothing more than the hallucinatory embodiments of the thought-forms born of the mental-content of the percipient; or, in other words, they are

the intellectual impulses which have assumed personified form in the after-death dream-state.

«Accordingly, the Peaceful Deities are the personified forms of the sublime human sentiments, which proceed from the psychic heart-center. As such, they are represented as the first to dawn because, psychologically speaking, the heart-born impulses precede the brain-born impulses. They come in peaceful aspect to control and to influence the deceased whose connection with the human world has just been severed; the deceased has left relatives and friends behind, works unaccomplished, desires unsatisfied and, in most cases, he possesses a strong yearning to recover the lost opportunity afforded by human embodiment for spiritual enlightenment. But, in all his impulses and yearnings, **karma** *is all-masterful; and, unless it be his* **karmic** *lot to gain liberation in the first stages, he wanders downwards into the stages wherein the heart-impulses give way to brain-impulses.*

«Whereas the Peaceful Deities are the personifications of the feelings, the Wrathful Deities are the personifications of the reasonings and proceed from the psychic-brain-center. Yet, just as impulses arising in the heart-center may transform themselves into the reasonings of the brain-center, so the Wrathful Deities are the Peaceful Deities in a changed aspect».

These visions, however, are not forever. They exist as long as the spirit goes through the «review-examination» of his life. Soon the movie ends and the spirit moves on to another after-death dimension or perhaps, rebirth into another physical body.

Mr. Evans-Wentz explains:

«From day to day the Bardo (after-death state) visions change; concomitant with the eruption of the thought-forms of the percipient, until their karmic driving force **exhausts** *itself; or, in other words, the thought-forms, born of habitual propensities, being mental records comparable as has already been suggested to records on a cinema-film, their reel running to its end; the after-death state ends, and the Dreamer, emerging from the womb, begins to experience anew the phenomena of the human world».*

Thus we come to the next stage of after death life – what happens after the examination? Until now our sources have been quite in agreement on every point. Let us sum up these points.

1) The spirit leaves the physical body and continues to survive.

2) It exists now in a subtle body that has special powers.

3) It is met by friends, relatives, guides, guardian angels, or beings of light.

4) It then passes through a period of examination in which it reviews its way of life.

5) It then proceeds on to a variety of after-death states.

G) AFTER DEATH STATES
THAT FOLLOW THE EXAMINATION

As to what happens now, we have varying points of view. Regardless of the varying views however, all agree that there are after-death states in which one can rest or pass through various types of experiences. The type of environment a spirit may find itself in is again a function of his mental state. Our various sources are quite in agreement about that.

This after-death state will be a function of how an individual has lived his life. According to St. Antonios, the spirit passes through its examination and then is shown the after death states, both pleasant and unpleasant, and finally «it» (the soul is neither male nor female) is placed in one of those after-death states to wait until the final Judgment Day, after which it will enter into heaven or hell. The after-death state it will experience will be in accordance with the way it has lived his life. If it has been a loving, unselfish, correct type of person, who has done to others as it would have liked others to do to it, it will find itself in a pleasant after-death environment awaiting the Judgment Day. If on the other hand, it was an unloving, selfish, incorrect type of person, who had no regard for others, it will find himself in an unpleasant after-death environment.

It is rather commonly accepted, even by Christian Theologians, that these after-death states are not actually places but rather mental states which are dependent on the individual's character and way of life. This has been evinced in the previous comment by theologian Meletis expressing the ideas of St. Gregorios of Nissa.

Islam too, embraces that these after-death states are mental creations. According to Iqbal, «*Man creates his own reward and punishment. There is no such thing as Heaven and Hell. Heaven and Hell are states, not localities. Their descriptions in the Koran are visual representations of an inner fact, i.e. character*».

This reminds us of the words of Christ in Luke 17.20:

«*The kingdom of God does not come in such a way as to be seen. No one will say "look, here it is", or "there it is", because the kingdom of God is within you*».

If the kingdom of God is within us, then it must be a state of mind and not a locality; a state of mind which is full of love and purity.

Of our twelve sources, Christianity and Islam as official organizations do not consider the possibility of the spirit reincarnating. The rest of these sources (with the exception of Moody's and Osis' research, which do not touch this subject), state that there are after-death states in which the spirit may rest, or pass through various experiences (again according to his character), but that if the spirit has not perfected itself in its expression on the earth, that it must eventually return to a new body and personality and continue with the school of life.

Socrates embraced this concept with great faith. His belief goes something like this:

1) The spirit who leaves the body, with many desires and earthly needs, will be attracted towards the earth and will experience lower and more unpleasant after-death states.

2) It will wander restlessly in these lower after-death states until such a time that it can become born again and continue on with its attempt to satisfy its earthly desires.

3) The wise or pure spirit has no difficulty in making the journey to Hades, where it enjoys the company of like-minded souls.

4) But even these souls in Hades do not remain forever, they too have to return to the school of life.

Socrates described these after-death states in terms of rivers and lakes, i.e., the river of pain, the river of burning fire, the river of hate and the river of wailing.

It becomes apparent that the after-death state is not simply a place of silent resting, but rather a place of kinetic activity and experiences. **Theologian Meletis** comments on this in his book *What Happens After Death.*

«There the soul finds the epitome of happiness, the fulfillment of all its virtuous desires. It is neither a rest or relief from the sufferings of life, nor a state of immobility and stagnation, nor the Buddhistic Nirvana, nor the Elesian Field of antiquity, nor the Islamic paradise of harems and rice heaps.

«The soul lives eternally moving, continuously discovering the endless Divine riches. At every moment new glorious divine rays are unveiled. The glory and the grandeur of God create supreme satisfaction without ever causing satiation. The view of the Divine grandeur is the ultimate blessing for the soul».

The *Tibetan Book of the Dead* explains that there are six possible states that a spirit can enter into after the examination period (if it does not manage to become enlightened). They are called the six lokas or states of being:

1) The Deva Loka or the "world of the angels" and the heaven for those who have performed many good actions.

2) The Asura Loka or the "titan world" or the "world of the fallen angels" who are in opposition to the forces of good.

3) The Human Loka where the spirit takes on another human body and continues with its evolution.

4) The Brute Loka or the "incarnation into the lower aspects of the human race," as an individual with little self-awareness or spiritual inclination.

5) The Preta Loka or the "world of ghosts" where the spirit gets lost wandering close to the physical dimension, obsessed with having some contact with the physical world, i.e. lost in its own reality.

6) The Hell Loka or the "dimension of extremely unpleasant experiences."

It is understood that all of these lokas are **temporary** dwelling places. It is also understood that they are relative and unreal in the absolute sense. Our only permanent reality is **pure consciousness** and these states and experiences are simply taking place in our pure consciousness as events take place in space. It seems that evolution takes place basically on the human level, and that spirits must return over and over to that level in order to gain experiences and proceed with their evolution.

As the spirit is about to move on to one of these lokas, the subtle body begins to lose its old characteristics and takes on the characteristics of the new body it will wear in the new dimension. This new body will have some old characteristics but will, in addition, have new qualities that are necessary for the learning of new lessons.

The **Hindu** concept is very similar to this. The spirit may achieve one of the various lokas or heaven states according to its tendencies and character. Good actions, worship and love will achieve an after-death state in the higher paradise heavens of pleasant experiences. If, however, the soul has not realized the highest truth of oneness with God, it will have to return to life in a physical body and continue to work towards self-realization.

It is possible, however, for a soul with great love and devotion to a form of God, i.e. Jesus the Christ for Christians, or other forms for other religions to achieve the **Brahma Loka** or the kingdom of God where it will remain until the dissolution of the universe, at which time it will merge with God. That process is called Krama-mukti or «slow liberation» where the spirit does not reach final liberation, but does not need to continue with further incarnations on the earth. It is «God's guest» as it were, until the dissolution of the universe or «Judgment Day».

In Jiva-Mukti, or liberation while living, the spirit reaches union with God, the universal spirit, immediately upon overcoming all identification with the body and mind, and is absorbed in the consciousness of God as its own inner self.

We might imagine that when Jesus spoke about the Kingdom of Heaven, He was referring to the Brahma Loka where they would reside with Him until the final day of the dissolution of the universe. The personalities who are not able to have such intense devotion have to return to earth – perhaps a good simile for hell. It may be useful to briefly mention at this point that some people believe that Jesus **did** in fact teach the concept of reincarnation and that it was accepted by some of the early church followers. It seems that around 536 A.C., a church council was held in Constantinople that was controlled by Emperor Justinian and his wife Theodora. Apparently at this church council parts of the Bible referring to the preexistence of the spirit before its incarnation into the body and the concept of reincarnation were deleted.

There were many dubious and seemingly incorrect activities surrounding this council in which the Pope himself was Justinian's prisoner for some days. The Pope himself rejected the decisions of the council. A number of books have been written lately concerning this subject and are available for the reader who desires to investigate more deeply.

Regardless of these deletions that may have taken place, there remain passages in the Bible that are difficult to explain without the concept of reincarnation.

1) Why did Jesus say that St. John **was** Elias? How could he be Elias if he was not a reincarnation of Elias?

2) Why did the apostles ask whether the man born blind was born that way because of his own sins or because of his parents' sins? How could he have sinned before he was born, if he had not lived another life previously? This means that the apostles must have at least believed in the possibility of reincarnation in order to ask the question.

3) In the Bible, Jesus cured people by telling them that their sins are forgiven. If physical handicaps are the result of past sins, how can people be born with such handicaps unless they have sinned in previous existences?

4) Jesus frequently declared that, «As you sow, so shall you reap» and «He who lives by the sword, will die by the sword»; clearly stating the law of karma. But we do not see this happening in one lifetime. We see a number of very ethical and selfless persons receiving what, to our eyes, appears to be outrageous injustice.

On the other hand we see people with very selfish and unethical behavior, getting away with atrocities. Thus, either Jesus' words do not apply to all situations, or there is some past and/or future, which we do not see which balances these apparent injustices. Perhaps in past or future lives?

Let us continue with our investigation of the after-death states. Seth emphasizes that the after-death states we encounter will be dependent on our particular belief system. He explains that some belief systems help us to feel more relaxed in the after-death state and give us a structure in which we can work through these experiences. Otherwise the mind might become too disoriented.

«Certain images have been used to symbolize such a transition from one existence to another, and many of these are extremely valuable in that they provide a framework with understandable references. The crossing of the River Styx is such a one. The dying expected certain procedures to occur in a more or less orderly

fashion. The maps were known beforehand. At death, the consciousness hallucinated the river vividly. Relatives and friends, already dead, entered into the ritual, which was a profound ceremony also on their parts. The river was as real as any that you know, as treacherous to a traveler alone without proper knowledge. Guides were always at the river to help such travelers across.

«It does not do to say that such a river is illusion. The symbol is reality, you see. The way was planned. Now that particular map is no longer generally in use. The living do not know how to read it. Christianity has believed in a heaven and a hell, a purgatory, and reckoning; and so, at death, to those who so believe in these symbols, another ceremony is enacted».

Mr. Evans-Wentz agrees with this concept as indicated in his commentary on the *Tibetan Book of the Dead*:

«Accordingly for a Buddhist of some other school of thought, as for a Hindu, or a Moslem, or a Christian, the Bardo experiences would be appropriately different; the Buddhist's or the Hindu's thought-forms, as in a dream state, would give rise to corresponding visions of the deities of the Buddhist or Hindu pantheon; a Moslem's visions of the Moslem Paradise; a Christian's visions of the Christian Heaven, or an American Indian's visions of the Happy Hunting Ground. And similarly, the materialist will experience after-death visions as negative and as empty and as deityless as any he ever dreamt while in the human body. Rationally considered, each person's after-death experiences, as the Bardo Thödol teaching implies, are entirely dependent upon his or her own mental content».
Let us take a look at how some of Moody's subjects experienced after death realities.

One woman had this experience while she was temporarily clinically dead:

«And after I floated up, I went through this dark tunnel... I went into the black tunnel and came out into brilliant light... A little bit

later on I was there with my grandparents and my father and my brother, who had died... There was the most beautiful, brilliant light all around. And this was a beautiful place. There were colors – bright colors – not like here on earth, but just indescribable. There were people there, happy people... People were around, some of them gathered in groups. Some of them were learning...

«Off in the distance... I could see a city. There were buildings – separate buildings. They were gleaming, bright. People were happy in there. There was sparkling water, fountains... a city of light I guess would be the way to say it... It was wonderful... But if I had entered into this, I think I would never have returned... I was told that if I went there I couldn't go back... that the decision was mine».

A man who died of a heart attack, and then was revived, had this experience:

«All of a sudden I was just somewhere else. There was a gold-looking light, everywhere. Beautiful. I couldn't find a source anywhere. It was just all around, coming from everywhere. There was music, and I seemed to be in a countryside with streams, grass, trees and mountains. But when I looked around - if you want to put it that way - they were not trees and things like we know them to be. The strangest thing to me about it was that there were people there. Not in any kind of form or body as we know it; they were just there.

«There was a sense of perfect peace and contentment and love. It was like I was part of it. That experience could have lasted the whole night or just a second... I don't know».

These experiences seemed to be representative of more pleasant experiences of light that tend to be present in the early after-death stages. It seems, however, that these images do not last and that we eventually move on to more important business, i.e. our evolution. According to Seth:

«A belief in hell fires can cause you to hallucinate Hades' conditions. A belief in a stereotyped heaven can result in a

hallucination of heavenly conditions. You always form your own reality according to your ideas and expectations. This is the nature of consciousness in whatever reality it finds itself. Such hallucinations, I assure you, are temporary.

«Consciousness must use its abilities. The boredom and stagnation of a stereotyped heaven will not for long content the striving consciousness. There are teachers to explain the conditions and circumstances. You are not left alone, therefore, lost in mazes of hallucination».

H) CHOOSING THE NEXT STEP IN OUR EVOLUTION

According to most of our sources, once we spend some time in these after-death states, we must then decide on our next step in the evolution progress as we work towards self-perfection. For most of our sources this means reincarnating into another physical form in order to continue with our learning process.

Seth explains that there are also other possibilities:

«Before the time of choosing, there is a period of self-examination; there will be emotional ties with other personalities whom you have known in past lives, and some of these may supersede your relationships in the immediately past life. This is a meeting place for individuals from your own system also, however.

«All necessary explanations are given to those who are disoriented. Those who do not realize that they are dead are here told of their true condition, and all efforts are made to refresh the energies and spirits. It is a time of study and comprehension. It is from this area that some disturbed personalities have those dreams of returning to the physical environment».

This reminds us somewhat of Walter Cowan's experience in which he was read the record of his previous lives before being allowed to return to the physical body under the guidance of Sai Baba. Seth goes on to explain that there are three basic possibilities at this point:

«You may decide upon another reincarnation. You may decide to focus instead upon your past life, using it as the stuff of new experience, as mentioned previously creating variations of events as you have known them, making corrections as you choose. Or you may enter another system of probability entirely; and this is quite apart from a reincarnational existence. You will be leaving all thoughts of continuity of time behind you in such a case».

Thus, the choices are:

1) Simply, to reincarnate.

2) To reevaluate our previous existence, replaying some of the events over and over so that we may practice with more evolved ways of reacting. It is like making dress rehearsals before the actual show, which will take place later on earth. Or it might be like solving practice questions which we have failed at in the previous examination (previous life), before we return to earth for reexamination.

Seth explains that this second option is a preparation for the next life:

*«If you find severe errors of judgment, you may then correct them. You may perfect, in other words, but you cannot again **enter into that frame of reference** as a completely participating consciousness...*

«Some choose this rather than reincarnating, or rather as a study before a new reincarnation. These people are often perfectionists at heart. They must go back and create. They must right their errors. They use the immediately-past life as a canvas, and with the same «canvas», they attempt a better picture. This is a mental and psychic exercise undertaken by many, demanding great concentration, and is no more hallucinatory than any existence».

3) The third possibility of entering other *«systems of probability»* is available only to those who have sufficiently perfected themselves through the various reincarnation lessons. They have learned the basic lessons of **love and self-knowledge**. According to Seth:

«Some simply find the physical system not to their liking, and in such a way take leave of it. This cannot be done, however, until the reincarnational cycle, once chosen, is completed, so the last choice exists for those who have developed their abilities through reincarnation as far as possible within that system.

«Some, finished with reincarnation, may choose to reenter the cycle acting as teachers, and in such cases some recognition of higher identity is always present. Now there is an in-between stage of relative indecision, a midplane of existence; a rest area, comparatively speaking, and it is from this area that most communication from relatives occurs. This is usually the level that is visited by the living in projection from the dream state».

The explanations given by theosophy and the writings of **Alice Bailey** are amazingly similar to these of Seth. According to Alice Bailey, the following process takes place after the spirit leaves the body:

1) We have already described the way in which the energy body withdraws itself and leaves along with the mind and other more subtle bodies.

2) Then a review takes place in which the spirit sees its life before it in one moment like a map. Moody's subjects confirm that this review takes only a few seconds.

3) The spirit then isolates the three main conditioning factors of that life. In this way the qualities of the three grosser bodies – physical, vital, emotional – are expressed in the form of seeds, or key qualities, which will determine to a great degree the qualities of the future body and mind. These key factors represent the basic qualities of the physical, energy and emotional bodies.

4) The spirit then moves on into the company of those close to it in likeness and prepares for the second death.

5) The second death is of the emotional-mental body. Here the spirits tend to experience different environments according to their type.

a) The emotional types find themselves in an astral environment that is cloudy and unclear, full of emotional vibrations, as is a mind that is clouded with chaotic emotional movements.

6) These spirits will experience a slow attrition of the emotional body as the emotional disturbances and attachments run slowly out, because there is no longer any stimulation from the senses and body identification.

b) The spirits of the emotional-mental type tend to withdraw from the emotional body, dwell in the mental body, and destroy the emotional body with the will.

c) The mental type may call on light from the soul or higher beings to remove any emotional disturbances, and then destroy the mental body through the use of mantras or prayers or concentration on higher aspects of his own being (i.e. Om, Gayatri mantra, Lord's Prayer, Lord Have Mercy).

7) Of course any mantras or prayers that will be used on those levels will have to be learned here on the earth level first. Any particular effort, which we make here on this level, will be of great advantage to us in the after-death state.

8) Then the spirit begins to organize its forces for reincarnation deciding on through whom it will incarnate and what characteristics it will manifest in this incarnation.

9) It organizes its energy body and the process of reentry begins.

10) It chooses its sex, the time and place of birth, its parents and the various major experiences of that coming life, knowing that therein lie the lessons it needs to continue its spiritual evolution.

I) WHERE DO THESE
AFTER-DEATH ENVIRONMENTS EXIST?

Before going on to discuss the various factors affecting the reincarnational choices, let us first consider for a moment where these after-death environments exist. We have already affirmed through our many sources of information that these states are *states of mind* and not localities. States of mind are not limited by time or space.

This has been evinced by Dr. Moody's subjects who just thought of another place and then found themselves at that place. Mental states are independent of time and space and there can be as many different mental states in a room as there are different people. Seth explains to us that our concept of time and space is limited and false in the ultimate sense.

«These after-death environments do not exist necessarily on other planets. They do not take up space, so the question, «Where does all this happen?» is meaningless in basic terms.

«It is the result of your own misinterpretations of the nature of reality. There is no one place therefore no specific location. These environments exist, unperceived by you amid the physical world, but you are unable to tune in to their ranges. You react to a highly specific but limited field. As I mentioned earlier, other realities coexist with your own. At death, for example, you simply divest yourself of physical paraphernalia, tune into different fields, and react to other sets of assumptions.

«From this other viewpoint, you can, to some extent, perceive physical reality. However, there are energy fields that do separate them. Your entire concept of space is so distorted that any true explanation is highly difficult.

«Now what your senses tell you about the nature of matter is entirely erroneous, and what they tell you about space is equally wrong – wrong in terms of basic reality, but quite in keeping of course with three-dimensional concepts. (Humorously): In out of body experiences from the living state, many of the problems are encountered, in terms of space, that will be met after death. And in such episodes, therefore, the true nature of time and space becomes more apparent. After death it does not take time to go through space, for example. Space does not exist in terms of distance. This is illusion. There are barriers, but they are mental or psychic

barriers. For example, there are intensities of experience that are interpreted in your reality as distance in miles».

Thus it appears that we are limited by time and space only while we are limited by the physical body. According to Seth our after-death activities could be taking place right in our own living room.

«After-death you may find yourself in a training center. Now **theoretically,** *this center* **could** *be in the middle of your present living room, in physical space, but the distance between you and the members of your family still living – sitting perhaps, thinking of you or reading a paper – would have nothing to do with space as you know it. You would be more separated from them than if you were, say, on the moon.*

«You could perhaps change your own focus of attention away from the center, and theoretically see the room and its inhabitants; and yet still this distance, that has nothing to do with miles, would be between you».

Perhaps the example of the radio or television would help us to understand how it is possible for more than one dimension to exist in the same location. In the room where you now are sitting there are the hundreds of voices and images which have been emitted by radio and television stations. You cannot perceive them. If however, you turn the radio or the television on, you will be tuning into a completely different reality. If you change the station, you will perceive even another reality. All of these realities exist in the same space, without interfering with each other. In the same way the various material and nonmaterial dimensions exist in the same space without interfering with each other.

Just as we can turn the radio on and change the focus of our reality, there may be techniques with which we can tune into other dimensions and through which those other dimensions can tune into our reality.

This does not exclude the possibility that an after-death dimension might also exist somewhere else in the solar system or even in the outer spaces of the universe. In order to understand this we must relinquish our narrow concepts of time and space, which nuclear physics has recently exposed as mental constructions which help us to organize our lives on earth, but which have no ultimate reality.

Some spirits who have great attachments to certain earthly objects, situations or persons may become confused after leaving the body and try to interact with the physical environment. These are usually less developed spirits who live in ignorance of their spiritual nature and have a great emotional attachment to the earth. These are lost souls who are being held up in their spiritual evolution because of their attachment to the earth plane. The *Tibetan Book of the Dead* explains this situation. The word "Bardo" in the following text refers to the state between death and rebirth:

«It is said that the retardation of a Bardo-bound Spirit may be for any time from 500 years to 1000 years; and in exceptional cases, for ages. All the while, because escape from the Bardo being prevented, the deceased can neither pass on to a paradise realm nor be born in the human world. Ultimately, however, the womb will be entered and the Bardo will come to an end».

The state in which the spirit finds itself is the Preta Loka where it wanders lost in its own subjective reality unable to continue on with its examination and after-death states or to reincarnate. This is the result of the soul's attachment to the Earth level. Guides will eventually be able to communicate with these lost souls and bring them to the truth. We too may help them by encouraging them to follow the beings of light who come to them to help them.

Setn sheds some light on the subject:

*«Now, You may after death utterly refuse to believe that you **are** dead, and continue to focus your emotional energy towards those you have known in life.*

«If you have been obsessed with a particular project, for example, you may try to complete it. There are always guides to help you understand your situation, but you may be so engrossed that you pay them no heed.

«...Large fields of emotional focus toward physical reality can hold you back from further development. When consciousness leaves the body, and is away for some time then the connection is, of course, broken. In out-of-body states, as in a dream, the connection still holds. Now it is possible for an individual who has died to completely misinterpret the experience and attempt to reenter the corpse. This can happen when the personality identifies almost exclusively with the physical image.»

There need be **absolutely no fear** of unfortunate spirits who might be caught in this state. They can do us no harm. The only way in which they can affect us is to create fear in us. We have nothing to fear but fear itself. On the other hand we can help them and influence them positively. We can pray for Christ to shine His light on them, for guardian angels to come and guide them out of their state. We can even talk to them with love and logic explaining to them that they cannot stay here on the Earth plane, and that they are suffering unnecessarily. We can guide them to let go of their attachment with the earth and follow the guides who are coming to take them to higher, more beautiful dimensions, assisting them with their evolution. This loving advice will surely help to heal their problem and set them free to continue with their journey.

J) CHOOSING A NEW INCARNATION

Alice Bailey has humorously pointed out that «Death, if we could but realize it, is one of our most practiced activities. We have died many times and shall die again and again».

As we have mentioned earlier, all of the sources (except organized Christianity and Islam) accept the concept of reincarnation (Moody's and Osis' studies do not touch the subject). Let us now take a look at some of the factors which may affect the process of reincarnating.

We have already mentioned that according to Alice Bailey, the spirit determines which lessons are necessary to learn, and begins to form a new energy body and personality, and chooses the parents through which it will incarnate.

Psychiatrist **Helen Wambach** asked her 750 subjects under hypnosis to go to the point before birth and discover if they are choosing to be born and whether they are being helped with this decision. Eighty one percent of the subjects answered that they chose to be born. The other 19% were unaware of any choice or had no clear answer. Of those who chose to be born, 59% felt the help of counselors, who advised them concerning the choices at hand. Here are some of their answers:

1) «*Yes, I chose to be born, and there seemed to be a board or committee - a group of authorities to help me choose. I was not too anxious or interested in living this lifetime, but I knew I had something to do on this plane, something to accomplish. The whole feeling of birth seemed to be an annoying, unpleasant trip to accomplish something in this lifetime. I felt an urgency*». (Case A-408)

2) «*When you asked if I chose to be born, I didn't want to, but I was convinced by a counselor that I needed to help with enlightenment. The man who helped me choose seemed to have a white beard and cane and was a kind of spiritual guide.*

«*When you asked about the prospect of being born, I became clearly aware that I didn't want to and was very reluctant. I even knew that I had tried to abort while in the womb*». (Case A-434).»

These subjects were from a cross-section of social groupings with no special tendency towards spiritual matters. They were, on a whole, quite surprised by their apparent reluctance to be born. A full 68% felt negative about the idea of being born, while 26% felt enthusiastic about being born. This is a very surprising result to be found in a society that fears death and is so attached to life in the physical body.

Here are some more cases:

3) «*Yes, I chose to be born. I had a very strong sensation of flowing from my expanded, dispersed self down into my physical center, and had a vision of it. I think someone helped me choose, but if they did, it was prior to the space I experienced, because I felt my own*

pressure to enter physical reality. My feelings about the prospect of being born were very positive and I was impatient to begin».
(Case A-349).

4) «Yes, I chose to be born, although I felt it was going to be a hassle. Someone helped me choose, someone more knowledgeable than I. My feelings about living the coming lifetime were that it was something that had to be done, like washing the floor when it's dirty». (Case A-285).

5) «Yes, I chose to be born, but somewhat reluctantly. Others were helping me choose and they seemed to be vague figures. Some were human shapes and some geometric shapes. There was a general agreement among all of us that it was somehow necessary, but I felt pushed into it». (Case-491).

6) «Yes, I chose to be born. I was waiting to return. No one actually helped me choose, but an old man was with me while I was making the choice. My feeling about the prospect of being born was that I was waiting and anxious to see if the body would be okay this time. This experience was very strange for me».

This last case is of particular interest because during hypnosis this woman realized for the first time that she was the same spirit who had previously incarnated through the same parents as her older sister who had died only after a few months. Now she was attempting to come back to the same parents and was *«anxious to see if the body would be okay this time».*

Let us now consider some of Seth's teachings concerning the preparation necessary before choosing a new incarnation.

«The time of choosing is dependent upon the condition and circumstances of the individual following transition from physical life. Some take longer than others to understand the true situation.

«Others must be diverted by many impeding ideas and symbols as explained earlier. The time of choosing may happen almost immediately in your terms, or it may be put off for a much longer

period while training is carried on. The main impediments standing in the way of the time of choosing are, of course, the faulty ideas harbored by any given individual.

«A belief in heaven or hell, under certain conditions, can be equally disadvantageous. Some will refuse to accept the idea of further work, development, and challenge, believing instead that conventional heaven situations are the only possibility. For some time they may indeed inhabit such an environment, until they learn through their own experience that existence demands development, and that such a heaven would be sterile, boring, and indeed, «deadly».

«Then they are ready for the time of choosing. Others may insist that, because of their transgressions, they will be cast into hell, and because of the force of such belief, they may for some time actually encounter such conditions. In either case, however, there are always teachers available. They try to get through these false beliefs.

«In the Hades conditions, the individuals come somewhat more quickly to their senses. Their own fears trigger within themselves the answering release. Their need, in other words, more quickly opens up the inner doorways of knowledge. Their state does not usually last as long, therefore, as the heaven state.

«Either state, however, puts off the time of choosing and the next existence. There is one point I would like to mention here: in all cases, the individual creates his experience. I say this again at the risk of repeating myself because this is a basic fact of all consciousness and existence. There are no special «places», or situations, or conditions set apart after physical death in which any given personality **must** *have experience.*

«Suicides, as a class, for example, do not have any particular «punishment» meted out to them, nor is their condition any worse a priori. They are treated as individuals. Any problems that were not faced in this life, will, however, be faced in another one. This applies not only to suicides, however.

«A suicide may bring about his own death because he rejects existence on any but highly specific terms chosen by himself. If this is the case, then of course he will have to learn differently».

It appears that spirit is free to choose the pattern of its reincarnational process. A spirit may choose to experience all the various religions, races, professions and social classes throughout its many lives, or it may decide to follow the same line of development in one life after the other. Seth communicates on this here:

«Now many personalities have extraordinary talents along specific lines, and these may show up again and again in succeeding existences. They may be tempered, used in various combinations, and yet overall still remain a personality's strongest mark of individuality and uniqueness. While most people adopt different trades, occupations and interests, for example, throughout the reincarnational cycle, with some there will be a very noticeable line of continuity. It may be broken occasionally, but it is always there. They may be priests or teachers, for example, almost exclusively».

The final goal or purpose for these many incarnations is to develop greater love and more expansive understanding and experience of our true spiritual nature; or in the words of Socrates, **self-knowledge.**

In religious terms it means Union with God, a relinquishing of identification with the personal self and merging the individual spirit into the Cosmic Spirit that we call God. One stage along this path is the experiencing of ourselves as multidimensional beings including our other reincarnational personalities and even other dimensions that we are not aware of. As we begin to identify more with our multidimensional spiritual nature, then we identify less with the particular body and personality we are temporarily occupying. This passage from **Seth Speaks** may help us understand this more quickly.

«First of all you must understand, again, that now you do not realize your true identity. You identify instead with your present ego, so when you think in terms of life after death you really mean

a future life of the ego that you know. At the end of reincarnational cycle you understand quite thoroughly that you, the basic identity, the inner core of your being, is more than the sum of your reincarnational personalities.

«You might say that the personalities then are but divisions of your self **here.** *There is no competition between them. There never was any real division, but only a seeming one in which you played various roles, developed different abilities, learned to create in new and diverse ways. These reincarnational personalities continue to develop, but they also understand that their main identity is also yours.*

«When the cycle is finished therefore, you have complete knowledge of your past lives».

This process of repeated reincarnation offers the spirit the continuous opportunity to evolve spiritually through the various earthly life forms in order to once again merge with the one God from which it has originally come.

It is a circular journey from the **one**, through the diverse many, back to the **one**. This poem by the Sufi poet **Jalluddin Rumi** beautifully expresses this concept:

«I died as mineral and became plant,
I died as plant and rose to animal,
I died as animal and I was man.
Why should I fear? When was I less by dying?
Yet once more I shall die as man, to soar
With angels blest; but even from angelhood
I must pass on: all except God doth perish.
When I have sacrificed my angel soul,
I shall become what no mind e 'er conceived.
Oh, let me not exist! For Non-existence
Proclaims in organ tones: «To Him we shall return».

With this understanding of the purpose of reincarnation, let us take another look at some of the answers given by Helen Wambach's hypnotized subjects:

7. *«Yes, I chose to be born, and I was helped in the choice by a council of souls. My feelings about the prospects of living the coming lifetime came through that I knew my parents needed me because they had lost a fifteen-month-old girl in a fire. So I felt eager to come to them». (Case A-48)*

8. *«No, I didn't choose to be born. There was someone insisting that it was time to return. I felt very reluctant to live another lifetime because it was very pleasant on the cloud. But a voice was insisting that I needed additional experience». (Case A-277).*

We return over and over for additional experience, to learn to love and work on creating more harmonious relationships.

9. *«Yes, I chose to be born, but with reluctance. There seemed to be friends around me as I chose, saying, «Oh, come on, it will be good for you». My feelings about the prospect of living the coming lifetime were that there was lots of work ahead, especially work on my relationship with my mother». (Case A-142).*

10. *«No, I didn't choose to be born. I had the feeling that something or someone controlled my birth, but I couldn't understand any more about it. I didn't want to go through another lifetime again, but I felt like I needed to learn to love. I felt like it was a recurring lesson and I had to come back again and again and again». (Case A-394).*

11. *«I was very resistant to the idea of choosing to be born, but I know I had to make the decision myself. My feelings about the prospect of living another lifetime were that it was really a drag. This surprises me because I love living so much». (Case A-301).*

It may be interesting to summarize the statistical results of Psychiatrist Helen Wambach's research on the 750 hypnotized subjects. Consider that these results are coming from a Christian society that has no programmed beliefs about reincarnation.

1) 81% chose to be born.

2) 59% felt the help of counselors.

3) 26% felt enthusiastic about being born.

4) 68% felt negative about being born.

5) 64% chose their particular sex.

6) No one felt the true inner self to be male or female before the creation of the embryo.

7) 87% recognized people in their present lives to be spirits with whom they had relationships in
previous lives.

8) 89% experienced separateness from the embryo until the 6th month of development.
9) 86% experienced the emotions of the mother before being born.

10) 95% were able to recall one or more past lives.

11) 90% found the death experience in those past lives to be a pleasant experience.

12) Almost all found the birth experience to be unpleasant and in some cases disgusting, shocking and painful.

These are truly amazing results coming from the subconscious memory of a society which celebrates birth and mourns death; from a society which doubts life after death and reincarnation; from a society which denies and fears death.

It makes us think that perhaps the truth is other than what we have been lead to believe all these years.

K) THE BIRTH EXPERIENCE
Let us take a look at some of the birth experiences as described by

Helen Wambach's subjects:

1. «*The birth-canal experience for me was slow torture. I had a feeling of being crushed – there was not enough room – pain, and pressure. After I was born I felt the cold and that there was too much light. There was pain especially in my head and face. I was aware of other people's feelings. My mother had a feeling of relief from pain, but also some disgust. There was indifference on the part of all the hospital attendants, except for one warm-hearted nurse*». *(Case A-143).*

2. «*In the birth canal I was still just next to the body, but then I was in it and then out of it and could observe. After I was born I felt wet and I know I had a bloody forehead, that I was bruised. I was aware that someone in the room said I looked funny. That somehow bothered me and would stay with me, even though I also heard them say I would be okay later*». *(Case A-182).*

3. «*The birth-canal experience for me wasn't smooth, but in jerks, surrounded by softness. It was almost unyielding though. I remember the tremendous bursting desire to breath and feel my limbs free, to stretch. After I was born, the first breath seemed burning and almost painful, and I was coughing and shaking. Before being washed my skin was burning and painfully being tightened by drying ambiotic fluid and itching. Unfortunately, I was scrubbed by some idiot with a horrible scratchy sponge. It was a very cold delivery room. Everyone was quite aware of my mother's feelings about the birth. I kept hearing her say, «I don't want it, I don't want it*». *(Case A-348).*

4. «*When you asked about the birth canal, I felt very angry. I wanted to get out and my mother doesn't want me to get out. I'm kicking, fighting, screaming. After birth I have relief, but I'm still upset. My thought was, «So that's the place I wanted to get into so much!» I was aware of other people's feelings after my birth. My grandmother was very nasty. I first thought it was a snotty nurse, and then I realized it was my grandmother*». *(Case A-352)*

Through these answers, which are quite representative of the answers given by all the subjects of this study, we can see that we must be much more careful in our handling of the young infant. The spirit is recording the emotions of the mother and others even before it emerges from the womb.

The emotions, words and actions that surround the tiny infant are creating impressions on its relatively pure mind, thus forming its belief system and character. It is true that there will be some karmic tendencies already there from previous lives, but our attitudes and feelings will also have a great effect on this new human being.

L) CONCLUSIONS

We have started studying death as the final stage of life and we have ended up **with birth as the final stage of death**. It seems that as Socrates argued over 2000 years ago, it is only logical that since the dead come from the living, that the living must come from the dead. He argued that all of life passes through the evolution of opposites. Day becomes night and then again day. Thus the living pass on to the dead and then back again to living.

We started out studying how we may overcome the fear of **death** and in the end have found that **birth** is a much more traumatic experience. This too, is quite logical. All of the sources we have studied unanimously agree that the human being is actually a spirit that exists before birth and after death, in a subtle body which has many more dimensions of freedom than the physical body. It is able to fly instantaneously to any point in the universe. It can pass through objects. It is not limited by time and space.

Imagine which would be more pleasant; the process of death in which the spiritual being is released from the limitations of the physical body, or the process of birth in which this free expansive spirit is forced into the helpless little body of an infant who is at the mercy of its well-meaning, but unfortunately uninformed parents.

Unfortunately or fortunately, depending on how we want to look at it, we are forced over and over to return to the earth to continue with our lessons and our tests until we do it perfectly right.

According to Christ, we cannot enter into the kingdom of heaven until we are perfect. Do we know anyone who is going to make it? We come over and over learning how to love unconditionally and how not to be identified with this temporary vehicle of the body and mind.

Death is not to be feared. Neither should it be sought as a release from our responsibilities, pains or problems. For we will take with us any problems we have not solved and just recreate the same situation when we come back so that we may eventually learn to transcend the problem. Our problems are our lessons – our opportunities for growth on this earth.

An individual who faces death is ready to face life and live with full intensity every moment. In the next chapter we will examine how we can prepare ourselves so that we are ready for our own death, or the death of loved ones, whenever it may happen. And in the following chapter we will discuss how we may help others, who are close to death, face this moment more consciously, more peacefully and more spiritually.

As a result of this research into the various concepts of death held by the various religious and philosophical systems, we are left with the following circular model of the relationship between life and death. The picture we get is a circular one in which the spirit passes into life from the death state and back into the death state from the life state, and then back into the life state from the death state. When we die to the state of the body consciousness, we are born into the state of non-body consciousness. When we die to non-body consciousness we are born into body consciousness again.

Let us end this section with the following chart which indicates the results of this research into the various sources regarding death. This chart indicates to us where these different sources agree on the various after-death stages.

As we can see from the chart, all 12 sources agree on the first five aspects of the death experience:
1) That the soul exists after death.

2) That it exists in a subtle body.

3) That this subtle body has special powers unlike the physical body.

4) That the soul is met by other souls who guide it through the death transition.

5) That the soul must pass through an examination of how it has lived its life.

Source	Spirit Lives	Has energy body	Has Powers	Meets beings	Life Exams	Other Dimensions	Depend on Character	Chooses Incarnation	Purpose of Life to Love	Death is not to be feared
Christianity	Yes	Yes	Yes	Yes	Yes	Yes	Yes	No	Yes	Yes
Hinduism	Yes	Yes	Yes	Yes	Yes	Yes	Yes	Yes	Yes	Yes
Buddhism	Yes	Yes	Yes	Yes	Yes	Yes	Yes	Yes	Yes	Yes
Islam	Yes	Yes	Yes	Yes	Yes	Yes	Yes	No	Yes	Yes
Theosophy	Yes	Yes	Yes	Yes	Yes	Yes	Yes	Yes	Yes	Yes
Socrates	Yes	Yes	Yes	Yes	Yes	Yes	Yes	Yes	Yes	Yes
Alice Bailey	Yes	Yes	Yes	Yes	Yes	Yes	Yes	Yes	Yes	Yes
Seth	Yes	Yes	Yes	Yes	Yes	Yes	Yes	Yes	Yes	Yes
Dr. Moody	Yes	Yes	Yes	Yes	Yes	Yes	Not Refer	Not Refer	Not Refer	Yes
Dr. Osis	Yes	Yes	Yes	Yes	Yes	Yes	Not Refer	Not Refer	Not Refer	Yes
Kubler Ross	Yes	Yes	Yes	Yes	Yes	Yes	Not Refer	Yes	Yes	Yes
H. Wambach	Yes	Yes	Yes	Yes	Yes	Yes	Yes	Yes	Yes	Yes

Concerning aspect number six, that the spirit then exists in after-death dimensions until the next step, it is agreed upon by all sources except the studies of Dr.s Moody, Osis and Kubler-Ross, which did not investigate this subject. Thus they do not mention this point.

That these after-death states are a function of how a person has lived, thought, and behaved in life is affirmed on by all sources except the last four that simply do not mention this point because it is outside the scope of their studies.

That the soul chooses a new incarnation is affirmed by 8 out of the 12 sources. It is not mentioned by Dr.s Moody and Osis, since this is beyond the scope of their studies. The clergy of Christianity and Islam generally do not accept the concept of reincarnation. On the other hand there is no part of the Bible, or the Koran, in which Christ or

Mohammad declare that there is no such thing as reincarnation. There are sections in these books, however, which could be interpreted in favor of the concept of reincarnation.

That the purpose of life is to learn and to love and that death is nothing to fear is agreed upon by all the sources.

The question about what happens after death will never be satisfactorily answered for each individual until he or she has a direct experience of the process of leaving the body. But until such a time when we may have that experience, it seems foolish to continue fearing that it may be something horrible when there are so many different sources verifying the same message **that it is simply the departure of the immortal soul from its temporary physical vehicle.**

Thus, death appears to simply be a more extended period of sleep in which we wake up in a new body rather than the same one. It is not, however, the void sleep that we might imagine. It is as active as our sleep state is here on earth today, but we simply are not able to bring the memory of these activities to our conscious mind.

Death to life is birth to the next dimension and death to the other dimension means birth to this level.

When we die from death, we come into life.
This brings to mind the heart-inspiring chant sung at the Greek Orthodoxy Pascal Resurrection mass.

Christ Is Arisen From the Dead,

He Has Conquered Death With Death.

CHAPTER II

FACING OUR OWN DEATH

OVERCOMING THE FEAR OF DEATH
BY FACING LIFE

(«People who have learned to live are not afraid to die»)

We seldom know on a conscious level when we or our loved ones are going to suddenly (or slowly) leave the physical plane. Thus it would be sensible to be ready at every moment for this possibility.

In the Bible we have the parable of ten virgins who were waiting the arrival of the bridegroom. Five virgins had plenty of oil to light their groom's way, while the other five did not think to gather enough, leaving him in darkness when he finally arrived. This is symbolic of our being ready for the Lord when our time comes to meet Him. Most of us are caught totally unprepared when the time comes – we feel that we are not ready, that we need more time to finish projects, to enjoy our lives, to work out our relationships and satisfy various other needs and desires. **The individual who is always ready for death is also always ready for life.**

Elizabeth Kubler-Ross, who had more contact with dying people than perhaps any other researcher believed that **«People who have learned to live are not afraid to die».**

In this chapter we shall explore some of the ways in which we can adjust our lives and ways of thinking so as to be always ready for death, whether it be our own or that of a loved one.

A) TIME WASTE IS LIFE WASTE

Satya Sai Baba says that «Time Waste is Life Waste».

We would feel very sad if we were informed that we will be soon leaving the physical body and might feel that we have not lived our lives in the way we wanted to or should have. We would desperately want to «buy more time», but this is seldom possible. We might also feel remorse because of having wasted our lives on vain pursuits and having ignored that which was really meaningful to us.

Following are a few examples of how Dr. Moody's patients changed their way of thinking and living as a result of having died and returned to life:

«I try to do things that have more meaning, and that make my mind and my soul feel better. And I try not to be biased and not to judge people. I want to do things because they are good, not because they are good for me. And it seems that the understanding I have of things now, is so much better. I feel like this because of what happened to me, because of the places I went and things I saw in this experience».
Many found these experiences a blessing that changed their way of life:
«It was a blessing in a way, because before that heart attack I was too busy planning for my children's future, and worrying about yesterday, that I was losing the joys of the present. I have a much different attitude now».
Others experienced a change of focus in their lives from the physical to the mental level:
«I was more conscious of my mind at the time than of the physical body. The mind was the most important part, instead of the shape of the body. All my life, it had been exactly reversed. The body was my main interest and what was going in my mind, well, it was just going on and that's all. But after this happened my mind was the main point of attraction, the body was second - it was only something to encase my mind».

Satya Sai Baba encourages us to use the memory of the fact of our physical mortality to help us keep our thoughts, words and actions in line with our spiritual purpose in life.

«Remember death. The body is the car in which you are riding to death. You may meet death any moment while riding. Some tree or lorry, culvert or such will bring it about. If you remember that time is running out every moment, you will not be tempted to waste time in idle talk or vain pursuits, wanton mischief or vulgar entertainment».

If we live with intensity, moving steadily towards our goals, we will always be ready for death when it comes. If we give sufficient attention to our mental and spiritual evolution, we will be more at peace with death when it comes. **The only possession we take with us is our character.**

The after-death state is not a solution for the lazy person who wants to avoid the difficulties and responsibilities of life. Neither does death release us from any negative tendencies or problems.
Socrates was of the belief that death is not a release from any tendencies or weaknesses of character. According to Socrates, our character followed us whenever we went. It appears that the «spiritual evolution» which we talk about is in reality the evolution of character throughout the various lives. This character is manifested as various positive and negative tendencies recorded in the "causal body" or what we might call the soul memory.

We incarnate over and over, working on correcting and purifying our character, attempting to mold it into a more divine shape with qualities such as love, peace, truth, selflessness, righteous action, non-violence and higher wisdom. It is the development and purification of this character that is our basic goal on earth. It is precisely these qualities of divinity that link one life with another.

We develop our character in three basic ways:

1) Through our moral conduct – doing to others as we would like them to do to us.

2) Through spiritual disciplines such as prayer, meditation, fasting, control of breath, etc., which increase our awareness and level of consciousness.

3) Through fulfilling our «Dharmic role» in the evolutionary process here on earth; and, through fulfilling our purpose or role in life.

Let us consider this last point in more detail.

B) WE HAVE COME TO EARTH WITH A PURPOSE

We each come to this earth for specific reasons, with specific roles to play, lessons to learn and goals to attain. If we do not work towards the fulfillment of these roles, lessons, or goals, we will never feel fulfillment and will not feel ready for death when it comes. We have an obligation to manifest our inherent abilities here on this earth. Seth emphasizes this point:

«Now: For those of you who are lazy I can offer no hope: death will not bring you an eternal resting-place. You may rest, if this is your wish, for a while. Not only must you use your abilities after death, however, but you must face up to yourself for those that you did not use during your previous existence».

Perhaps this is why Jesus cursed the fig tree that was not bearing fruit. We have come to this earth to develop and manifest the divine talents that are latent within us. Each of us has a specific part to play in this drama of life. Each of us is a unique component in this great machine called humanity. Each of us is a unique cell that has its own particular function in the body of humanity.

No individual is inherently more important than another. No work or function is higher or lower than another. The heart cannot function well if the stomach does not function well. The circulation cannot be efficient if the intestines do not do their job. The head cannot arrive to its destination if the feet and hands do not perform their purpose.

We come to this earth over and over playing various roles, pleasant and unpleasant, famous and insignificant (to human eyes), mental and physical. If we try to avoid playing the part for which we have come, we will be in continual conflict with our inner selves and never find peace or contentment.

This part which we have come to play is called our «Dharma». Each of us must seek to find our dharma in this particular incarnation. We must try to understand why we have come to this earth. What goals do we hope to fulfill before leaving these physical bodies? We must investigate our deepest inner feelings and uncover what our goals are on the personal, family, social, professional, national and global level. What would we have liked to have accomplished before leaving this physical body?

After listing these goals, the next step is to analyze and evaluate the way in which we spend our time and live our lives. Are we working efficiently towards the fulfillment of these goals, or are we wasting our time and energies on chasing other, less important pursuits or in routine, mindless, habitual, robot-like functioning?

We can come to conclusions as to which types of efforts and activities we would like to increase in our lives and which we would like to decrease. It is not important to actually arrive at our goal before we die, but rather to feel that **we are living our lives in accordance with our goals**, and that we are doing everything that we reasonably can at the moment to move in that direction. If we feel that our beliefs, words and actions are all in harmony with our goals, then we are able to leave our physical body peacefully.

Making these changes in our lives means facing and transcending the many attachments, aversions, fears and social conditioning which prevent us from discovering our real goals in life; and, once finding them, from being able to dedicate ourselves to them. These attachments and fears control our mental states, imprisoning us in a wall of fearful ignorance, very much like Plato's cave. We must break these chains and ascend into the light of the realization of our purpose here on this earth.

We will know when we have found our dharma – i.e. our part to play this time around – by the satisfaction, fulfillment, joy and meaning it will give us. If we do not enjoy what we are doing, then we have not found our real role yet. If we are bored or tired with what we are doing, then we must seek further, either to find what our real purpose is here on this earth, or to be able to see the divinity and beauty in what we are now doing. Thus we must either change what we are doing or change the way we perceive what we are doing so that we may be happy.

When we have found our dharma we are inspired by our role. We play it with intensity. It is our whole life, but at the same time, we remember that it is a *role* and not our true self. A time will come when we will leave that role and examine how we played it. Then we will be given another role. This changing of roles may take place within one lifetime or from one lifetime to another.

Some may complain that social and economic responsibilities do not allow them to work in their dharmic line. Christ has specifically promised us that **if we do the Lord's work** here on earth, then He will supply all our **needs.**

Psychiatrist Helen Wambach asked her hypnotized subjects for what purpose they chose to be born. What was the reason they took these physical bodies? Here are some of their answers:

«When I was choosing to be born, I was aware that one of my children was with me in this time between lives. I felt strongly that my purpose in this life was to produce a great leader, and that one of my sons would be a great leader who would produce social changes. I don't want my other children to know about this, and I wasn't aware of it until the hypnosis, that my strongest purpose was just to give birth to this son». (Case A-187).

What more beautiful a gift can an individual offer to the world than an enlightened human being who would add more love and wisdom to the world around him/her?

«When you asked the purpose, I felt strongly this life was chosen to experience rejection by my mother and sister, and my final

detachment so that I can get on with my spiritual tasks». (Case A-338).

Thus many of the unpleasant and apparently unjust reactions which we experience from those around us **are actually chosen by us** before birth as tests and opportunities to develop unconditional love and understanding.

«My purpose in this lifetime is to learn patience and love of my fellow man, and to relieve loneliness by mixing with other people, and showing compassion». (Case A-57).

«I think my purpose in this life is to learn humility – that everyone inside is the same – there is no better or worse. To show and teach this». (Case A-434).

«My purpose for this lifetime is to evolve from a me-feeling to a we-feeling, to accept responsibility, not to place any restrictions on other people. I am here in this time period to help with the transition». (Case B-82).

«My purpose is to overcome fear». (Case A-353).

«My purpose is to become free of materialism and to combat negativeness. To combine male and female emotions for control, love and strength». (Case B-25).

«My purpose for this lifetime is to learn humility». (Case A-46).

«I am here to learn, but also to teach and to help in this period of a transition in history from the religious to the scientific to the spiritual life». (Case B-88).

«My purpose for being born was to realize my own inner thoughts and independence. The time period was relevant to women's liberation because it was a time for women to find strength, influence and independence in a man's world». (Case A-454).

«I felt that this lifetime was chosen to experience abandonment, so *that I could learn self-sufficiency. I came in this time because this part of the twentieth century is very good for psychological growth, and I will develop my ability to teach and respond to others in this time period». (Case A-378).*

«When you asked the purpose, I realized it was to establish a new relationship with people I owed from damage I did to them in past lives. I am certainly aware now that my husband in this life is an alcoholic and I understand that I must help him because I was unkind to him in a past life». (Case B-11).

These inspiring answers fit in so well with the basic goal of the transformation of character. Through them we also come to the understanding that one of the main means of measuring our spiritual progress is the degree of positive feelings towards others – regardless of their behavior.

C) HARMONIZING OUR RELATIONSHIPS

Our degree of spiritual evolution can be measured by our ability to love. The degree of harmony in our interpersonal relationships is also a function of our ability to love unconditionally. Thus we can understand much about our strengths and weaknesses along the spiritual path by observing the degree of harmony or conflict we experience in our relationships with others.

We will attract to ourselves exactly the individuals and characters that have something to teach us. Our close family members and friends are chosen before we are born because we have much to teach and learn from each other. The relationship is destined in order to teach and learn from each other. The relationship is destined from before birth, but our reactions are our own free will.

For example, it may be fate that we will have to receive rejection from our close relatives. But how we will react to that rejection is up to our own free will. We can become hurt, angry and bitter, avoid all contact with them, and suppress our feelings; or, we can continue to love them unconditionally, realizing that the problem is theirs and not ours.

Thus the realm of personal relationships is a major field of learning here on the earth, especially for the emotionally-oriented individual. When a relationship is not going well, we will do well to examine ourselves for selfishness, immaturity, pride, lack of self-confidence and, most important of all, lack of love and self-acceptance. The disharmonies in our relationships will show us our weaknesses and where we have to develop more.

We decide, even before we come to this earth, to play these various roles with those around us so that we may all continue with our spiritual evolution. We may come over and over with the same spirits until we work things out with them.

There are three main attractive forces between people – love, hate and fear. These three emotions will attract the object of these emotions into our lives. It is better to attract what we love rather than what we fear or hate. So let us work on developing more love and transcending (not suppressing) hate and fear. And even if we do attract what we fear or hate, we can eventually overcome the problem by learning to love what previously repelled us.

Psychiatrist Wambach's subjects verified that they incarnated over and over with the same souls playing different roles. Consider some of these answers:

«My mother was my sister in a past life and my father was a lover. My first son had been a grandfather in one lifetime of mine, my second son had been a father, and my first daughter a friend. My second daughter I saw clearly as a mother of mine in a past life». (Case A-225).

«My mother was a close male friend from a past life. My father was my wife whom I used to treat cruelly in a past life». (Case A-460).

«I became aware that in one of my previous lives my mother killed both my father and myself. Neither she nor my father remember. I became aware, but somehow I always dreamed about this experience. Only now, as I see the relationships here in the hypnosis, I have freed myself». (Case A-589).

«My mother was a mother of mine in a past life and also a child of mine in a past life. My children told me they wanted to be my children before I was born, and I knew them not only from past lives, but from the between-life period». (Case A -381).

«I knew my mother had been my mother previously. I had been twins with my father, so we were very close, I was aware of numerous other family relationships that stem from past lives. I was glad to be a sister rather than a wife to my brother». (Case A-513).

«My mother was a sister or close relation in a past life. My father was a captain of a ship I was a sailor in. I got the impression that many other people who were in this life were in a particular lifetime of mine in the 1600's». (Case A-558).

«I realize now that part of my purpose this time is to be aware of my mother's feelings toward me and learn to love her anyway. Oh boy, is that a toughie!» (Case A-242).

«I came in this time period to correct past errors and to work out my guilt about certain relationships». (Case A-57).

«I came in this time period because certain other people I needed to work out relationships with would also be alive at this time». (Case B-70)

«I came this time to get to know my mother better who was my best friend in a previous life and she was alive in this time period». (Case B-55).

Psychiatrist Wambach's comments on these results are of interest to us.

«Among the 87 percent responding «Yes» to the question about knowing parents in past lives, there was an astonishing variety in the relationships reported. Fathers in this lifetime had been lovers in the past, mothers in the past, brothers, sisters, friends and children. Mothers in the current lifetime were seen as friends,

fathers, brothers, sisters, children. There was no consistency at all in the way in which people in this life were related in past lives. The Freudian hypothesis of daughters wishing that fathers were lovers was not evident in the data, nor did sons see their mothers as wives in past lives more frequently than seeing them in other relationships. Often parents in this life were friends or distant relatives in past lives.

«Mates and lovers were perceived as friends, close relations, parents from past lives as well as lovers. Some subjects did report that husbands or wives in this lifetime had been in a sexual relationship with them in past lives as well, so there appeared to be a trend for people to work out sexual relationships by assuming the same sex roles in several lifetimes. But again, this was well under one third of the reports of relationships in past lives to husbands or lovers now».

This data along with other available information generates some of the following thoughts.

1) We tend to incarnate over and over with some of the same souls.

2) We incarnate with the souls who have lessons to teach us or lessons to learn from us.

3) If we are unable to harmonize the relationship in one life, we will have to attract the same soul or the same type of personality in a future life and eventually learn the lesson.

4) It seems therefore logical and useful to try to harmonize our relationships now so that we may enjoy lives of greater love and harmony and, simultaneously, have a free conscience at the moment of death.

When counseling people who are about to die, I have noticed that death is much more disturbing to them when they have failed to reconcile their relationships with those around them. Also those who remain often feel guilt that a mother, father or sibling has passed on before they were about to «work things out with them», and now it is too late.

Isn't it better then to begin to take a look at our relationships **today** and discover where we are harboring anger, resentment, bitterness, jealousy, hate, fear or other separating emotions? If these people are available and open to communication, then we can begin to discuss our relationships with them with the hope of settling our differences, forgiving each other and starting a new relationship based on love and communication.

There also may be **positive emotions** of love, affection, respect, gratitude or admiration which we feel, but have never expressed to these persons. It would be a shame for one of us to leave before these positive emotions are expressed.

This is one of the basic steps which we must take if we are to be ready for death at any moment, whether it be our own or the death of another. If these other persona in your life are not available, or are not ready to listen or to communicate, then we can at least transform our own feelings. We can let go of all of our bitterness and other negative feelings, and **imagine the others surrounded by light and love and wish them well.**

We can forgive them for everything and clear up any negativity from our side. Then we will be able to leave our physical body much more peacefully, with less karma to drag us back down into the same unpleasant type of human interaction. Love and forgiveness are our basic tools here.

One simple exercise is to imagine that we are about to die in a few minutes and bring the various important people in our life to mind and think what we would like to express to them before we leave. We can write down our thoughts to these persons, as we imagine that we will not be seeing them again. Then we might want to give this letter or express these feelings to them personally.

If we owe anything to anyone, it is best to repay it and not leave debts standing. These debts will be like connecting chains, which will bind us again to the same situation. If we have harmed someone, it is best to develop humility and ask for forgiveness. If they don't want to communicate about it, we can relax our body and mind and imagine the scene in our minds and ask them for forgiveness in our imagination. We can also write a letter asking for forgiveness. This will clear us from the picture.

We may also ask God's forgiveness. God is always ready to forgive the sincere of heart. Lastly we must also **forgive ourselves** and not hold on to old guilt which makes us feel separate from God and others.

If we have difficulty thinking positively about someone, we can bring to mind five positive qualities that this person has. In this way we can change the image we have for this person. This will help to open our hearts.

The more we examine how we can prepare for a peaceful death, the more we realize that **preparation for death is in reality preparation for life**. It is like the relationship between sleeping and waking. If we have not lived our day in such a way so as to feel peaceful and satisfied at the moment of falling asleep, we will not be able to let go and will feel restless. Thus the next day will be even more unpleasant.

In the same way, if we do not live our lives in harmony with our inner beliefs, we will feel panic and remorse at the moment of death. Consequently, the next life will start out with those unpleasant vibrations. We start out where we have left off.

Dr. Moody's subjects who have died and come back to life verify that they were suddenly inspired to live much less selfishly.

1) «*I didn't tell anybody about my experience, but when I got back, I had this overwhelming, burning, consuming desire to do something for other people... I was so ashamed of all the things that I had done, or hadn't done, in my life. I felt like I had to do it, that it couldn't wait*».
2) «*When I got back from this, I had decided I'd better change. I was very repentant. I hadn't been satisfied with the life I had led*

up to then, so I wanted to start doing better.

Another subject saw one soul trying to communicate to those whom it had left behind to change their ways before it was too late.

Dr. Moody: *«Was there any particular thing she was trying to tell them?»*

Subject: *«Well, it seems more or less that she was trying to get through to them, trying to tell them, seemingly, to do things differently from what they were doing now, to change, to make a change in their lifestyle. Now, this sounds kind of put on, but she was trying to get them to do the right things, to change so as not to be left like she was. «Don't do as I did, so this won't happen to you. Do things for others so that you won't be left like this».*
I 'm not trying to moralize or make a sermon, but this seemed to be the message that she was trying to get across... It seemed that in this house there was no love, if you want to put it that way... It seemed that she was trying to atone for something she had done... It's an experience I'll never forget».

Theologian Meletis firmly believes that souls continue their relationship with the incarnated souls whom they have recently left.

«Does the departed Spirit have the power of communicating with its family, acquaintances and friends? Or does it cease to be interested and think about the people on the earth? There is no doubt whatsoever that there is intimate communication. The relationship is not severed by death. It simply changes. The bounds and mutual helping of one another between the living and the dead continue to survive. We are one spiritual body with Christ as our head. Our spiritual bonds are not broken, not even by death. The spirits of our loved ones are observing us, are interested in us, and struggle along with us in our pleasant and difficult tasks».
Perhaps the greatest obstacle toward our being able to transcend our emotional weaknesses and negative reactions towards others is the fact that we are so controlled by our attachments, aversions, fears, social programming and habit patterns. Self-examination is

one way in which we can observe and transcend some of these obstacles.

C) SELF-EXAMINATION

In reality, **we are being examined every moment of our lives**. Every experience is an opportunity that we can use for growth into greater awareness. We often fail to see the lesson in an experience because we do not have enough emotional freedom.

We would do well to identify with our inner spiritual nature that has existed as other personalities before its birth into this body and will continue after the death of this body. Then we will be freer to see the truth and "answer the questions" on the «examination of life» more correctly.

When we "answer" from the ego level, we are usually wrong. The ultimate question of life is "**who am I?**" The basic purpose of life is to answer this question, to realize our true spiritual nature, or to **know ourselves**. Socrates felt that it was better to die than not examine one's life continually. He was persecuted and eventually condemned to die because of his philosophical search and his encouraging others to do the same. Here he shows the conviction of his beliefs:

«If you say to me... you shall be let off, but upon one condition, that you are not to inquire... in this way any more, and that if you are caught doing so again, you shall die - if this was the condition, on which you let me go, I would reply: «...while I have life and strength I shall never cease from the practice and teaching of philosophy, exhorting anyone whom I meet... Are you not ashamed of heaping the greatest amount of money and honor and reputation and caring so little about wisdom and truth? The unexamined life is not worth living».

It is not enough, however, simply to examine our lives philosophically. This wisdom must become love and selfless action. It must become a feeling of spiritual oneness with all beings in the universe and bring harmony and peace into our lives.

E) TRANSFORMING OUR BELIEF SYSTEMS

As we examine more deeply into our personality through self-analysis, we will discover that, at the basis of our personal reality, we have a **belief system**. This belief system forms the structure of our lives and the various experiences that we encounter.

Our basic belief system filters out the information that flows in through our senses. It allows only those thoughts and impressions which are consistent with our belief system to reach the conscious mind. The rest is hidden away in the subconscious.

The examination and transformation of belief systems is a subject which requires a whole separate book and not a few pages. This subject is explained in detail in the book **The Psychology of Happiness.** Let it suffice to say that there are two basic core beliefs upon which all our other beliefs are based.

One core belief is that **I am this body and personality** and the other core belief is **I am an immortal soul**. Our goal is to strengthen the second belief system as it offers us much more inner security, self-confidence, strength, fearlessness, joy, peace and inner satisfaction in our lives. It is also obvious that we will not fear death if we firmly believe we are immortal souls.

One basic problem is that we are strongly affected by the collective belief system of the society around us and find it difficult to break free from it. It is true that our personal reality is created by our personal belief system, but in many cases our personal or spiritual belief system cannot become free enough from the socially accepted system. Thus we basically experience a reality based on the **social** system of beliefs which is working deep in our subconscious.

Thus we will be able to experience the result of our spiritual belief system either when our concentration becomes so strong that we are completely unaffected by what others believe or when the society as a whole evolves into this system of belief.

From early childhood many of us have been taught that we are souls; but the actions of our parents and of those around us may have shown us clearly that they did not believe this to any great depth. If we truly believed that we were soul, there would be no worry, anxiety, fear, sense of depression or helplessness, no bitterness or resentment – there would be only love and peace. Seth challenges us to experiment with a belief in good without a belief in evil.

«Quite simply, a belief in the good without a belief in the evil, may seem highly unrealistic to you. This belief, however, is the best kind of insurance that you can have, both during physical life and afterward.

«It may outrage your intellect, and the evidence of your physical senses may shout that it is untrue, yet a belief in good without a belief in evil is actually highly realistic, since in physical life it will keep your body healthier, keep you psychologically free of many fears and mental difficulties, and bring you a feeling of ease and spontaneity in which the development of your abilities can be better fulfilled! After death it will release you from the belief in demons and hell and enforced punishment. You will be better prepared to understand the nature of reality as it is. I understand that the concept does indeed offend your intellect, and that your senses seem to deny it. Yet you should already realize that your senses tell you many things, which are not true; and I tell you that **your physical senses perceive a reality that is a result of your beliefs.**

«Believing in evils, you will of course perceive them. Your world has not tried the experiment as yet which would release you. Christianity was but a distortion of this main truth – that is, organized Christianity as you know it. I am not simply speaking here of the original precepts. They were hardly given a chance, and we will discuss some of this later in the book.

«The experiment that would transform your world would operate upon the basic idea that you create your own reality according to the nature of your beliefs, and that all existence was blessed, and that evil did not exist in it. If these ideas were followed individually *and collectively, then the evidence of your physical senses would find no contradiction. They would perceive the world and existence as good.*

«This is the experiment that has not been tried, and these are the truths that you must learn after physical death. Some, after death, understanding these truths, choose to return to physical existence and proclaim them. Through the centuries this has been the way».

F) LEARNING TO LET GO - MEDITATION, RELAXATION, PRAYER

One of the ways in which we can soften the mind for the reshaping of the belief system is through daily practice of some mental discipline such as deep relaxation, mind control, prayer or meditation. In this way the mind is relaxed and becomes more malleable for self-transformation. It can then be filled with more positive qualities.

Death is a process of letting go of everything; a surrendering of the body and its attachments. It requires letting go of all the concerns which are occupying the mind – the projects, plans, relationships, business and professional concerns, possessions, pains, problems and even joys and pleasures. When we practice deep relaxation or meditation, we learn to let go of all these concerns and experience natural inner peace which is always present in our actions and even in our efforts.

We need to learn detached, effortless action, which is far more efficient and productive than tense, anxious, stressful effort. Thus, when the moment of death comes, we are able to face that experience in the same way: with peace, dignity and conscious awareness. We will have learned through our inner experiences that we are something above and beyond the body and mind. As a result we will concentrate our attention more on the spiritual aspect of our existence, which will eventually slip out of the body, and thus will be able to face death with inner peace. This does not mean that we will not try to live as long, and usefully as we can; but when the moment has obviously come, we will leave with a peaceful smile on our lips, meditating on the divine bliss of the spirit world we are about to meet. The first step then, is relaxation – letting go. The second step is focussing the mind on a higher entity or reality. Once we are completely relaxed we can concentrate our minds on the image or name of our chosen form of the Divine or we can imagine the Divine Light without form. It is said that if we have the name of God on our lips as we leave the physical body, then that name will carry us to a very high after-death state. This is only reasonable since we have already seen that the soul will automatically go to whatever place comes into the mind. Thus if we have God in our mind we will go to God.

Satya Sai Baba comments:
«Listening to some Puranic (scriptural) tales you might say that it is quite enough if the name of the Lord is remembered at the very last moment of life. But it is a difficult task to recall that name in the end if you have not practiced it for years. In the surge of emotions and thoughts that will invade you at the last moment, the name of God will be submerged unless you learn from now on to bring that name to the top of your consciousness whenever you want it.

«There was a shopkeeper once who was inspired by the tale of Ajamila. He decided to remember the name of God with his last breath by a shortcut. He named his six sons after various gods for he knew that he was bound to call on any one of them when he was about to die. The moment came at last, and according to program he called the Lord by proxy, six times in all.

«The boys came and stood around his cot and as he surveyed the group, the last thought that came to the dying man's mind, just when he was about to quit, was, «Alas, all of you have come away. Who will look after the shop now?».

«You see his shop was his very breath all through his life and he could not switch to God at short notice. The latent tendencies will have their say, whatever you may wish.

«It is no mean achievement to get the name of the Lord on one's tongue at the last moment. It needs that practice of many years,

*based on a deep-rooted faith and a strong character without hatred
or malice. The thought of God cannot survive in a climate of pride
and greed. Moreover, how do you know which is the last moment?
The God of death does not give notice of his arrival to take hold of
you. He is not like the photographer who says, «I am clicking, are
you ready?».*

*«If you wish your portrait to be hung on the walls of heaven, it must
be attractive; your stance, your pose and your smile must be all
nice, is it not? So be ready for the «click» day and night, with the
name of God ever rolling on the tongue and the glory always
radiant in the mind. Then, whenever «shot», your photo will be
fine».*

In his down-to-earth and humorous example Sai Baba makes us
realize the simple truth that **we will die in the way that we have
lived**. It will not be possible at the last moment to change our
character, interests and way of thought. This process must begin here
and now, through daily meditation and concentration on the name
or image of God or some other divine quality such as love or light.

According to the **Tibetan Book of the Dead,** we can prepare for
our death in five basic ways:

1) Commit to memory the fact that we are souls and that anything
that we see after death is simply a projection of our own mental
concepts.

2) Develop a communication and relationship with higher powers
through regular prayer.

3) Live our lives selflessly, serving others in any way that we can.

4) Practice special mantras or holy sounds which have the power to
dissolve the ignorance that binds the soul.

5) Practice of regular meditation in order to experience *pure
consciousness*, which is our true reality. Meditation in a way, is the
practice of dying. We die to the world of desires, senses and thoughts

so that we can experience the inner spiritual self, which continues after death.

According to the **Tibetan Book of the Dead**, *«To those who have meditated much, the Real Truth dawns as soon as the body and consciousness - principle part»*. The spirit is the consciousness principle that departs from the body and experiences its purity of self, because of the constant purifying effect of meditation.

We can practice positive projection and imagine ourselves to be souls and let go of the fears, tension and attachments of the physical body. We can repeat over and over inside ourselves: «I am a soul, I am a soul», «I am not this body, I am a spirit». In such way we can reprogram our falsely programmed minds.

G) FAITH IN GOD AND SPIRITUAL REALITY

In order to be able to really let go, we need to have a certain amount of faith in the truth of our spiritual nature and in the existence of God. Without the faith that nothing harmful will happen to us, it will be difficult to relax and let go. Faith in God is an all-covering shield against all the problems of life, i.e. fear, anxiety, worry, doubt, and a lack of security.

When we have faith in God, we fear neither life nor death, because we are sure that God will protect us in every situation. We may be tested and made to pass through various difficulties – but these are blessings in disguise. Through these tests, we grow more emotionally, mentally and spiritually mature. Faith in God is indeed a great asset when facing our own or another's death.

When we have such faith we attend to our responsibilities and leave all the results up to God. We make our greatest effort without being attached to the results.

Thus when the last moment comes, we feel that we have done our best and do not worry about whether we have succeeded or not; that is God's business. We have peace and contentment, knowing that we have done our best. We surrender the results.

H) DETACHMENT FROM THE
PHYSICAL BODY AND SENSES

The greater our attachment to the physical body and its needs, the more difficult it will be for us when we have to leave it. Our attachments, desires and sensual attractions will pull us downwards making death a difficult, painful and disturbing experience.

But this is not only true of death. These attachments and addictions also make life more painful and difficult, for we are seldom able to fulfill these desires and addictions as much as we would like and consequently, spend much of our time in discontentment and unhappiness.

It is said that *«the richest man is the man with the least desires, and the poorest man is the man with the most desires»*. The more simply we learn to live, the happier we are. All religions advocate simplicity or learning to control the desires of the body to a reasonable extent. Every religion offers us techniques such as prayer, fasting, spiritual retreating and various types of vows through which we can develop the power of will over our desire nature. This is an essential process if we want spiritual evolution or would like to be ready to face death at any moment.

A peaceful death requires our being to be able to let go our attachments and pleasures. If we are not ready to leave them, how will we be able to calmly face death? We will experience the pain of separation from our sources of enjoyment.

We come to the Earth over and over because only our body dies and not our ego. If our ego were to die, then we would be born spiritually and need not be born again. Then there is no need for reincarnating.

Jesus said, «Until a man be born again (spiritually), he cannot enter the Kingdom of Heaven». He also said, «Until a man becomes perfect, he cannot enter the Kingdom of Heaven».

The ways in which we can work towards this spiritual rebirth are basically four:

1) Through **love** for God and our fellow men.

2) Through **selfless service** to others.

3) Through **wisdom** of the truth of our spiritual nature.

4) Through the **control of the mind** and merging our mind in the Divine.

I) THE DREAM STATE AS A PRACTICE GROUND FOR AFTER-DEATH STATES

Just about everyone has had dreams in which they interact with deceased relatives or friends. In some cases this may simply be the workings of the subconscious mind. In other cases, we are actually communicating with these spirits in dimensions that are available to them and to us in our dreams. There appear to be many similarities between the after-death state and the dream state. In both dimensions the mind forms realities with its thoughts. We have the same powers in our dreams that we have after death. According to Alice Bailey, death is simply an extended sleep in which we wake up in a new body.

*«People are apt to forget that every night in the hours of sleep we die to the physical plane and are alive and functioning elsewhere. They forget that they have already achieved facility in leaving the physical body; because they cannot yet bring back into the physical brain consciousness the recollection of that passing out and of the subsequent interval of active living. **They fail to relate death and sleep.** Death is, after all, only a longer interval in the life of physical plane functioning; one has only «gone abroad» for a longer period. But the process of daily sleep and the process of occasional dying are identical, with the one difference that in sleep the magnetic thread, or current of energy, along which the life force streams, is preserved intact, and constitutes the path of return to the body. In death, this life thread is broken or snapped. When this has happened, the conscious entity cannot return to the dense physical body, and that body, lacking the principle of coherence, then disintegrates.»*

Seth not only agrees with Alice Bailey but also goes further to say that we might even be able to practice for after-death states by learning to consciously manipulate our dream reality.

«After-death experiences will not seem so alien, or incomprehensible, if you realize that you encounter similar situations as a normal part of your present existence.

«In sleep and dream states you are involved in the same dimension of existence in which you will have your after-death experiences. You do not remember the most important of these high adventures, and so those you do recall seem too bizarre or chaotic as a rule. This is simply because in your present state of development you are not able to manipulate consciously within more than one environment.

«You **do** *exist consciously in a coherent, purposeful, creative state while the physical body sleeps however, and you carry on many of the activities that I told you would be encountered after death. You simply turn the main focus of your attention in a different dimension of activity, one in which you have indeed continuously operated.*

«Now, as you have memory of your waking life and as you retain a large body of such memory for daily physical encounters, and as this fount of memory provides you with a sense of daily continuity, so also does your dreaming self have an equally large body of memory. As there is continuity to your daily life, so there is continuity in your sleeping life.

«This simple fact is that when you dream you are flying, you often are. In the dream state you operate under the same conditions, more or less, that are native to a consciousness not focused in physical reality. Many of your experiences, therefore, are precisely those you may meet after death. You may speak with dead friends or relatives, revisit the past, greet old classmates, walk down streets that existed fifty years earlier in physical time, travel through space without taking any physical time to do so, be met by guides, be instructed, teach others, perform meaningful work, solve problems, hallucinate.

«In physical life there is a lag between the conception of an idea and

its physical construction. In dream reality, this is not so. Therefore, the best way to become acquainted with after-death reality ahead of time, so to speak, is to explore and understand the nature of your own dreaming self. Not very many people want to take the time or energy».

Obviously, such an endeavor would take great time, energy, and a development of conscious awareness in the dream state. Carlos Castanenda's teacher Don Juan encouraged him to develop conscious awareness in his dreams by remembering to look at his left hand while in the dream.

Such techniques and tricks may be successfully used so as to bring about the ultimate goal of being able to discriminate between the witness and the body and mind which are experiencing the myriad changes of the physical, mental, emotional and dream worlds.

If we want to be the masters of ourselves, we will eventually maintain self-awareness not only in the waking and dream states, but even in the deep sleep state. When consciousness is maintained even in the deep sleep state, it is called «samadhi», nirvana, or in Christian terms, «ecstatic Divine Ground».

Thus the work we do on developing conscious awareness in our waking and dream states is useful not only for the after-death state, but also to the waking state and to our purpose here on earth which is self-realization.

J) CONCLUSION

Facing death and facing life are one and the same. If we learn to live harmoniously in accordance with our highest beliefs, we will die harmoniously in the same way. When we have no fear of life, we will not fear death. Ignoring death is not the way to ready one's self for it.

We can overcome our fear of death by becoming familiar with it, and by becoming familiar with our true selves. We can be ready at every moment to die peacefully, consciously, and spiritually by living in the following way:

1) Live our lives with intensity in harmony with our goals and ambitions in life.

2) Discover the purpose for which we have incarnated and work toward that purpose.

3) Seek to find greater **harmony in our relationships**, at least from our own part, through unconditional love.

4) Practice **regular self-examination** and always seek to improve the functioning of the personality, to discover our true spiritual nature.

5) Transform our belief system from "I am body" to "I am spirit."

6) Learn to **relax and concentrate** the mind through regular relaxation, prayer and meditation.

7) Live lives in **harmony with our conscience**. Do to others as we would like them to do to us.

8) Develop faith in, and love for, God.

9) Detach ourselves from the dependencies on the pleasures of the body.

10) Develop self-awareness in the waking and **dream state**, and learn to manipulate our dream reality.

Obviously preparing for death has nothing to do with retreating from life, but rather **living life more bravely** «like a warrior» as Don Juan suggests, always **remembering death to be waiting for us our left side**. In this way we are not tempted to waste time or energy on meaningless, vain activities, which do not improve the quality of our lives.

«Time Waste is Life Waste»

CHAPTER III

HELPING OTHERS
TO DEPART PEACEFULLY
AND CONSCIOUSLY

Since it is inevitable that we are all going to leave these physical bodies, we might as well depart with dignity and peace of mind rather than in conflict, fear and turmoil. Many great beings of history have faced death with great dignity, courage and peace of mind.

The moment of departure from the physical body also offers us a great opportunity for spiritual growth. It is a moment in which we have the greatest possibility of realizing our true spiritual nature.

In the previous chapter we have discussed how we can begin to live and think in such a way as to face death more consciously, peacefully and spiritually, without fear or conflict. In this chapter we will discuss some of the ways in which we can help others to make the same preparation, especially if they are close to death.

It is obvious, however, that we will not be able to help others to make changes and transformations which we have not made ourselves. Working on ourselves will be a prerequisite to helping others.

A) WE LIVE IN A DEATH-DENYING SOCIETY

Probably no other person in the western world has studied the process of death and dying as much as Psychiatrist Elizabeth Kübler-Ross, who worked with dying patients in hospitals all over the U.S.A. We might call her the first and foremost Western "thanatologist". She has done much to educate the doctors and nurses in American hospitals concerning the proper approach to a dying patient. Her valuable observations and conclusions can be found in her books: **On Death and Dying**, **Questions and Answers on Death and Dying**, and **Death, The Final Stage of Growth**. Let us consider some of her findings:

1) We live in a «death-denying society». Neither the doctors, nurses, patients, relatives nor friends are able to accept and face the fact of the mortality of the physical body. Thus we all try to ignore this reality.

2) As a result of her studies Psychiatrist Kübler-Ross has become convinced that there is life after death. She has openly declared in public lectures that for her, «It's not a matter of belief or opinion. I know beyond a shadow of a doubt».

3) She has also spoken in public with equal conviction concerning her belief in the reality of reincarnation.

4) Everyone knows the time of his or her death (at least subconsciously); thus it is seldom useful to hold this information from a dying person.

5) We are usually not able to hear or accept it when someone very emotionally close to us is trying to tell us that he or she feels that death is close. We ignore their message and try to cover it up with pleasantries so that we do not have to face this extremely painful reality. Thus we miss a valuable opportunity to communicate deeply with our loved one on a subject that may be dominating his or her mind.

6) Most people who have died and, for some reason, have come back to life, did not want to come back and would have preferred to stay in the after-death state which they found so much more pleasant than the incarnated state.

7) The people who had these death experiences no longer feared death after they returned.

8) Everyone who dies is met by a loved one who has proceeded before her/him into the life beyond. This loved one comes to guide and help the departing one through the transition into the out-of-body reality.

9) Dying does not have to be a lonely, isolated experience, but can be deeply shared with others who are mature and conscious enough to be able to share a wonderful experience, as the liberation of an immortal spirit from its physical confinement.

10) The departure from the physical body is probably the most beautiful experience of this life.

11) There are unseen, loving spirit guides within two feet of us at all times, so we never need to feel alone, or without help or support.

12) In the next dimension after death, there are different concepts of space and time.

13) After death, no one judges us, but we judge ourselves.

In her vast study of hundreds, perhaps thousands of dying patients who had to examine the value of their lives before dying, Kübler-Ross found two predominant purposes for living:

1) To be of service to others and not to live our lives satisfying only our own needs.

2) To learn to express love in all situations.

B) HELPING OTHERS TO LIVE UNTIL THEY DIE

Regarding the facilitation of people's dying process, Elizabeth said:

«Helping patients doesn't mean we help them to die, but that we help them to live until they die».
«People who have learned to live are not afraid to die».

Let us consider some of the ways in which we can help the dying person to be more peaceful and happy during his/her last days, before he or she departs for apparently more beautiful dimensions.

(We do not want to say here that the material plane is not also beautiful, or that it does not have the potential to become a really beautiful place if we would work towards it. We are simply reporting the evidence given by those who have died and returned – that as beautiful as this reality might be, the out-of-body world is even more beautiful. Neither are we recommending suicide or euthanasia, for each of us is here to learn very specific lessons, and until we learn those lessons, we are not karmically free to leave).

1) PRACTICAL CONSIDERATIONS

(**Note**: As the custom is to refer to the third person singular with the male pronoun, we will for convenience do so, but in each case we equally mean he or she, him or her.)

The first and most obvious help that we can give to a dying person is to help make arrangements for his practical needs and comforts. If the patient is able to face his pending death, he will want to arrange the details of his last will and testament. Besides that, there will be matters of insurance, details of how the family will continue without his presence, etc.

There may also be a need to find someone who can substitute him in professional responsibilities. The patient will be able to leave much more peacefully if he knows that his family and work responsibilities here on earth will be cared for in some way.

A patient, however, may not be able to face discussing these matters, and thus may not accept others' help. **He should not be pushed. No one should be pushed beyond his or her own limits in facing death**. Gradually, as the days pass, the inevitable will become more acceptable.

We will discuss shortly the psychological stages a dying patient passes through, as he approaches his departure.

2) FULFILLING NEEDS AND COMFORTS

We may ask, «Is there any thing I can do for you or to bring you that will make you more comfortable?» We are so often so overcome by depression with the fact that death is near that we forget that the person is still alive and has the ability to enjoy life.

He may want a book, some special music, or a favorite food. He may want to have contact with an old friend or with some special person. He may want to see his priest.

We may bring plants and peaceful music to his room. We may bring a musical instrument and sing together. He may want to see some slides, film or video which may be interesting to him. Any of these may or may not be interesting to the patient, depending on his psychological state. They should not be insensitively pushed onto a person who doesn't show interest.

3) HELPING HIM TO RELAX

The various mental conflicts, which permeate the mind of a person approaching death, often prevent him from being able to relax or even to sleep well. In addition there are often strong pains, or bodily difficulties, which increase muscular tension and prevent relaxation. The tension created by the pain creates more pain, which in turn, increases the tension in a vicious circle.

In many hospitals today patients are taught how to overcome pain through deep relaxation and concentration. By systematic, conscious relaxation of the muscles, the pain can be lessened or even eliminated.

The patient can also be taught to imagine healing energies and light penetrating the areas that are diseased, dysfunctional or painful, and begin to heal them or at least remove the pain with the power of the mind. Cassettes are available for helping patients learn such techniques.

Another way to help the patient to relax is with «co-meditational comforting breathing», which is a Buddhist technique in which we breathe with the other, guiding him to breath slowly as we make a sound "AAAAAAH" on his exhalation. He also may make the sound AAAAAH with you at first, until he tires and cannot continue. Then you can continue for him. You may also count his breaths on the exhalation, or say a prayer or mantra for him on his exhalation. In this way you are connected through the process of breathing for about twenty minutes. This helps the patient to transcend pain and connect with deeper states of inner peace.

4) MASSAGE, STROKING AND LOVING CONTACT

For those who know how to massage, this can be a wonderful way to relax and remove the pain for the suffering patient. If the patient is seriously ill, then you should be sure that massage is not contraindicated (i.e. harmful). Often when massage pressure might be contraindicated on the suffering area, it may be possible to bring relief by doing *reflexology massage* on the bottom of the feet for the corresponding area which we want relieve. Again you should know what you are doing, especially if the patient is seriously ill, or if there is any internal bleeding.

If you don't know how to give a massage, or feel that massage is not wise under the circumstances (a doctor can be consulted), then equal benefit can be achieved by simply stroking the patient in a loving way on the arms, legs, head or any other part of the body which you intuitively feel would be comforting for the patient.

Spiritual healing in which we place our hands on the person's chest, abdomen or forehead and *allow healing energies to pass through us from God to the patient* is of invaluable benefit for healing, relaxing, and even for passing out of the body peacefully. Simply place your hands where your intuition guides you and pray to God that His energies and love pass through you into the patient. Then let your mind be empty and allow the energy and peace to flow.

If it is best not to touch the body at all, then we can do the same allowing our hands to pass over the body about 1 to 3 inches from the body. It this way, we stroke and smooth out the *energy body*.

This is sometimes called "therapeutic touch" and is used in some hospitals by nurses. It relieves pain and speeds healing.

Simply holding hands or letting one's hand rest gently on the patient's body offers an opportunity for the transfer of love, energy and peace that the patient is greatly in need of. *There is no greater healing energy than love.* Many people are in hospitals and mental clinics simply because they have not had enough love and affection in their lives.

Loving contact can also be established through words, or even through the eyes. In the last days, less words are necessary and the patient may have his eyes closed more and more. In such times, our loving presence in the room is enough. We need not talk, nor necessarily make any kind of physical or verbal contact. We may sit silently and be peaceful and loving.

5) MEDITATION, PRAYER AND POSITIVE THOUGHT PROJECTION

As our friend, or loved one, begins to spend less time in the waking state and more and more in the sleep state preparing for his departure, we can sit silently and focus our minds in meditation or prayer. We can bring our minds to a state of pure peace. Then, if we like we may pray for the spirit who is about to be liberated. We may pray for a cure, for safe guidance, or we may simply visualize our loved one surrounded by white light. As he is surrounded with this white healing light, we may visualize the Christ or some saint or angel coming to help him. That help may enable him to get well and continue living some more years, or it may ensure that he will leave his body peacefully and proceed under the guidance of these beings of light, along the path of his spiritual evolution.

It is best to leave this decision to Divine wisdom, for we do not always know what is best for the spirit. Our personal desires and needs make us believe that it is always best to live. But that spirit's time may have come and it may be best for him to leave now. Our prayers for him to stay are often based on our own selfish needs and desires, and these prayers can prevent him from being able to leave.

It is best to surround him with white light and pray to God to help
him, and leave his fate (and ours) up to God. We may express our
preference that he be healed, but then we must leave the final result
up to His Infinite Wisdom. The purpose of life is not simply to live
— it is to **evolve**. Death is a very important step in the process of
evolution.

6) BE CHEERFUL, OPTIMISTIC & HAPPY

Our thoughts and feelings have a deep effect upon the people
around us. This is even truer of ill persons who are more sensitive,
open and easily affected by our thoughts and feelings. Even if we do
not express these thoughts and emotions verbally, the patient will
perceive them. Psychiatrist Richard Alpert who attended a seminar
by **Elizabeth Kübler-Ross** explains here how she brought this
point across to an audience of medical professionals. She asked
them:

*«How would you feel if you came into a hospital room to visit a
twenty-eight year old mother dying of cancer?» The answers
called out from the audience included: angry, frustrated, pity,
sadness, horror, confusion, etc. Then she asked us, «How would
you feel if you were that twenty-eight year old mother and
everyone who came to visit felt those feelings?» Suddenly it was
apparent to all of us how we surrounded such a being with our
reactions to death, and forget that there is a being just like us in
that body, who needs to make straight contact with someone».*

Thy dying or seriously ill patient has enough inner conflicts and
problems of his own, without adding our own fears, depression and
negative thinking. As much as possible we should try to strengthen
our faith in some basic spiritual beliefs:

a) We are immortal spirits and only the physical body «dies».

b) The soul that leaves the body is perfectly well after death, i.e.
much better than before.

c) We too are immortal spirits who have the strength to continue to live and even to be happy after our loved one leaves. We will certainly pass through some emotional pain due to the loss of this important person but we will, sooner or later, get over it and continue our lives. Why not let it be sooner?

d) All earthly events are happening according to **divine wisdom**, and thus no spirit can leave its body before its appointed departure time has come.

e) Life is always giving us exactly what we need in order to grow spiritually, even if it might be unpleasant. The pending death of our loved ones (whether he eventually gets well or actually dies) is a spiritual opportunity to develop emotional, mental and spiritual maturity and strength.

If we can remember these basic spiritual truths, then we will be able to be much more optimistic, cheerful and loving. We will have more love, energy and patience with which to help our loved one who is passing through such an internal crisis. We will have much more to offer in terms of emotional support if we ourselves overcome our negative emotions.

We should, however, avoid false happiness, or "empty smiles." We should not act out emotions that we do not truly have. If we connect with those spiritual truths, we will be naturally optimistic and peaceful.

7) STAYING AT HOME VS. STAYING IN A HOSPITAL

It seems rather obvious that if it is at all possible, a person would prefer to spend his last days in the peaceful loving environment of his home. Although hospitals offer the advantage of emergency medical help, they leave much to be desired in offering the patient the conditions he needs to die with dignity, self-respect, peace and love. Elizabeth Kübler-Ross, who worked daily in hospitals, firmly agrees. She makes the following comment about hospital environments:

"He may cry for rest, peace and dignity, but he will get infusions,

transfusions, a heart machine, or tracheotomy if necessary, He may want one single person to stop for one single minute so that he can ask one single question - but he will get a dozen people around the clock, all busily preoccupied with his heart rate, pulse, electrocardiogram or pulmonary functions, his secretions or excretions but not with him as a human being. He may wish to fight it all, but it is going to be useless fight, since all this is done in the fight for his life, and if they can save his life they can consider the person afterwards. Those who consider the person first may lose precious time to save his life!

At least this seems to be the rationale or justification behind all this - or is it? Is the reason for this increasingly mechanical, depersonalized approach our own defensiveness? Is this approach our own way to cope with, and repress, the anxieties that a terminally or critically ill patient evokes in us? Is our concentration on equipment, on blood pressure, our desperate attempt to deny the impending death which is so frightening and discomforting to us that we displace all our knowledge onto machines, since they are less close to us than the suffering face of another human being which would remind us once more of our lack of omnipotence, our own limits and failures, and last but not least, perhaps our own mortality?"

At home a dying patient can have his favorite meals, which in many cases, may give him the incentive to eat that which he needs in order to gain strength and perhaps get well. He will be surrounded with comfortable, friendly, warm and loving vibrations that will positively influence his state of mind and therefore his state of health. There will be less people walking in and out of his room, less noise and less disturbances throughout the day.

This, of course, may not be true of all home environments; some may not be conducive to health and peace of mind. Also, some illnesses just cannot be handled in a home environment, either because complicated instrumentation is necessary, or because there is just no one at home capable of tending to the patient's needs. Regardless of these facts, most patients would most likely like to spend their last days in the familiar environment of their home and leave with peace and dignity, rather than to become just another corpse in a mechanized and impersonal hospital.

In many cases, the **length of life is not nearly so important as the quality of life**. Each dying or seriously ill person and his family will have to decide these matters for themselves.

C) THE PSYCHOLOGICAL STAGES
ONE EXPERIENCES AS HE FACES DEATH

According to Elizabeth Kübler-Ross there are five basic psychological states which an individual may pass through as he faces his death. It is not necessary that each person will pass through all these stages. Some of the earlier stages may be skipped, while some of the latter ones may not even be achieved before the person departs. Some patients may experience more than one of these stages simultaneously.

She also points out that all of us go through these stages when we experience the loss of anything important in our lives. For example, we too, go through the same stages when we are about to lose a loved one, or any other loved object such as a house, a job, a car, or anything else which might be important to us.

1) STAGE I : DENIAL

The first reaction to the «bad news» is to deny its validity. The person is unable to accept this fact. The shock is too great and he or she protects himself or herself by denying it to be true. He may seek out other medical diagnoses in order to find someone who will verify his denial.

A person in this state is perfectly capable of ignoring obvious facts and medical tests. He is able «not to believe» the most expert medical advice, and is not at all interested in discussing death, or any matters practical or spiritual, which may be related to it.

This denial acts as a buffer that allows the individual to adjust inwardly so that eventually he can openly deal with this most unacceptable reality. This type of reaction usually appears in the early stages, when the patient has just been informed of the probable closeness of death. We use the word «probable» because no one can ever be sure when a person will die. Many people have been told they had one year to live, and have lived ten or twenty more years. Miracles do happen.

This reaction of denial occurs more frequently when the patient is informed by a doctor or someone not so closely related to the patient. The denial rarely continues until the end. Most patients manage to pass through it onto the other stages. This need to avoid the truth is sometimes dependent on the need for denial on the part of the patient's relatives and friends. If they are not able to handle accepting the situation and facing it, he too is handicapped in his psychological progress.

We must remember that all those who are extremely close to the denying patient will also be going through these stages. They are losing something they love and depend on, just as he is – life on this earth.

What should our reaction be during the denial stage? We must allow the patient the freedom to continue with the denial stage as long as he needs to, in order to prepare for the next stages. We may, however, give occasional hints that we are able and ready to face the situation whenever he is. Without pushing him in any way, we can occasionally test his willingness to examine the possibilities of the reality of his impending death. We may also look for his hidden and subtle clues that he would like to talk about his feelings about losing all these people, things and situations that he loves and is attached to.

Until the patient is able to open up to the reality of the situation, we can look for other ways in which to make him cheerful, such as bringing him interesting books, music or other activities. In some hospitals they have arts and crafts programs so that those who are able can use their time creatively making things.

2) STAGE II : ANGER

When the individual is no longer able to deny the possibility of his impending departure, he is often filled with a certain resentment, bitterness and feeling of injustice which may express itself as anger. He finds it completely unfair and unjust that he, who has tried so hard, who has conducted his life properly, who is still so young, who has not yet had a chance to enjoy the fruits of his efforts, who still has responsibilities to perform, must now suddenly and so quickly leave all this behind, and proceed to the unknown world of death.

He has worked so hard to create certain situations in his life, whether it is money, a house, car, projects, dreams for the future, etc. And now all these seem to be disappearing as if he is waking up from a dream or perhaps entering a nightmare. He is disappointed, frustrated and angry with the world, with his doctors, with his family. He is angry with God, who could be so cruel as to allow this to happen. Many in fact, lose their faith in God at this time. They cannot accept that a just God would allow such unjust things to happen.

This is true not only of those who are about to die, but also of those who are losing or have lost a loved one. They become angry with God, and often doubt His existence and the existence of a Divine Plan, that can allow such injustice to exist.

But this kind of vision is rather shortsighted and subjectively distorted. We are forgetting some basic spiritual realities:

a) The spirit continues after death and exists in an environment much more pleasant and rewarding than the earthly environment that it is leaving.

b) We, as spirits, have decided even before we entered into these bodies when we would be leaving them. It is our own past and present actions that determine our moment of death; not some mean and insensitive God sitting in Heaven.

c) Death is often a spiritual blessing both for he who is leaving and for those who are left behind. He who is leaving will be free of the spiritual blindness created by the physical body. Those who are left behind are being tested emotionally, mentally and spiritually as to how much faith and inner strength they have. They will grow stronger by now finding the **inner** security to replace the outer security they are losing as their loved one leaves them. The lost security or pleasure they once found through their loved one must now be found within themselves or in their relationship with God.

d) Divine Wisdom is seldom understood by the average mind. It must be accepted on faith. Gradually, as we evolve spiritually, and the blinding effect of material attachment decreases, we are able to see the beautiful wisdom of this incredibly intricate plan, which always gives us exactly what we need in order to grow spiritually. We will seldom see this truth when we are passing through these difficult tests, but years later we may realize the truth of the statement that «**A problem never comes to us without a gift in its hand**».

Regardless of these particular truths, the patient and his loved ones will find it difficult not to feel some moments of anger at the seeming injustice of it all. This causes the patient to become rather aggressive and demanding, argumentative and seldom satisfied with whatever one may do for him. In a way he is saying, «I'm still here, I haven't died yet – pay **attention to me**». He may not say it in these words, but basically he wants attention. His anger is not about a particular issue or anything we might have done or not done. He is angry about his situation and simply needs a place to discharge his frustration. The most likely targets are his loved ones, and the doctors and nurses.

How can we react to our loved one when he is in this state? The first thing we must do is to consider ourselves in his position; to imagine that we are him and that we are about to lose all these things we have loved, dreamed of, and worked so hard for. Immediately our compassion and patience will increase.

He needs attention, patience and love. We can simply listen to his negativity and perhaps even accusations without reacting. This may be enough. He may find release in just being able to express his complaints to someone. This, for us, will be a great spiritual opportunity to not identify with our egos, and not take anything that he might say personally.

We can imagine that he is talking about someone else and thus not get our ego involved. We may also practice *active listening* – a technique in which we try to deeply understand what our loved one is feeling. We continue to «feed back» to him what we believe we hear him saying in order to confirm what he means. This kind of communication can often help the patient get a clear look at his feelings and work through them. Basically, in this stage our loved one needs an opportunity to communicate with someone who is not emotionally involved, and who is patient, loving and compassionate.

3) STAGE III : BARGAINING

For most, the stage of anger gradually passes. At that point the dying person may enter into the bargaining stage. Here he tries to bargain in two basic ways:

a) He bargains with the doctors and loved ones in order to be allowed to have some last pleasurable and enjoyable experiences; even though these activities may be counter-productive to the therapy in process.

b) He may try to bargain with God for more time to fulfill his goals and desires before he finally has to leave.

When our loved one wants to enjoy some last activities before leaving the physical plane, we can try to do whatever is in our power to help him, as long as these activities do not seriously impair his chances to get well again. He may want to eat a favorite but now forbidden food, or go on a journey to a place he has always wished to see, or visit someone he loves dearly. We cannot underestimate the healing power of pleasant and happy experiences. *Laughter and love are more healing than many drugs*. The patient often has an inner, intuitive wisdom as to what is good for him, and we should respect that.

When the dying person is interested in seeking more time from God, we can use this excellent opportunity to help him develop greater contact with, and faith in, God. We can pray together with him each day. We can teach him how to relax his mind and concentrate it on imagining the divine healing light energy into his body and flowing to the organs which need healing. We can help him to visualize his chosen form of God and to feel a closeness or union. We can read to him case histories of people who have cured themselves through faith in God or through positive mental projection techniques.

A cassette can be created which will guide the individual into deeply relaxed states and towards positive mental visualization or communication with the Divine. (Available from www.HolisticHarmony.com)

4) STAGE IV : DEPRESSION

If the bargaining doesn't seem to be bringing results, the patient may soon enter into the stage of «depression» as he finally faces the fact that most probably he will soon be leaving his body. According to Kübler-Ross there are two types of depression:

a. Reactory Depression which is based on not being able to perform certain functions or responsibilities. For example the patient may be depressed that he is not able to earn money for the family, or look after the children or the business or some other function. In response to this type of depression, our best action is to try to help to find **practical solutions** to these problems.

We can try to find ways in which this person can fulfill these functions from his bed in spite of his illness. This is sometimes the preferable solution because it allows the patient to feel useful and gives him more incentive to live. If it is not possible for him to continue fulfilling his responsibilities, then our next goal is to find a way in which they can be performed by someone else. Then at least the patient will be able to relax knowing that his responsibilities will be cared for.

This type of depression is based on a concern for the others and what will happen to them. The other kind of depression is based on the unpleasant feeling of losing everything and requires a different type of reaction.

b) Preparatory Depression is a natural type of unhappiness based on the fact that the patient is now experiencing many losses. He may have lost practically all his money on hospital and medical bills. He may feel that he has lost his dignity, his job, and is about to lose his spouse, children, parents, relatives, friends, possessions and even his physical body. This depression is a preparatory stage in which he gradually faces these losses and learns to accept them. If he does not face them and experience the pain of separation from them, then he will never be able to enter the last stage of accepting what was previously unacceptable.

In this stage he does not need to be «cheered-up» but rather allowed to face, experience and live his pain; so that he may eventually accept it. We may listen, nod our head, sympathize with his condition, and share his pain of separation from all that he has loved and depended on for his sense of security, happiness and meaningfulness in life.

He will gradually pass through this preparatory depression and arrive to the stage of acceptance. In these latter stages, our presence and loving contact through meaningful eye contact and gentle strokes are much more important than superficial conversations.

5) STAGE V : ACCEPTANCE

After passing through the depression, the patient is usually tired. He may be more relaxed and perhaps weaker both physically and mentally. His energies are not so much directed toward holding on to life any more but rather more towards making a smooth and peaceful departure. He begins to prepare himself, to detach himself from those around him. He wants less contact with people– first with those less close to him – and gradually his circle of contact gets smaller and smaller. Towards the end he may choose only one or two very close loved ones as his only remaining contacts.

His circle of interest diminishes on all levels. He is not so interested in the material world and what is going on in it any more. He feels more and more distant from all those happenings. He, in many cases, will begin to have experiences of the world to come. He may pass over in his dreams and experience the wonderful after-death states. He may be visited by spirit forms of loved ones who have passed away and are now coming to help him with the transition.

He may prefer to sleep more and more or simply begin to stare off into space. He may not want to talk so much any more. At this time he needs more non-verbal communication. He may dose off to sleep, and we may sit there with our hand on his, or stroke his forehead, or simply sit silent enjoying the deep peace and serenity of a person who has entered this state.

We may sit in meditation and visualize the white light surrounding and protecting him. We may pray to God to help and guide him. When he opens his eyes, we are there with a smile, saying with our eyes, «I love you, I am with you, don't worry about anything».

If he wants to talk about his experiences, it might be enjoyable for all concerned. He may have news from relatives who have passed on. These contacts will bring peace not only to the dying patient but also to us, who will have our faith bolstered by these spiritual contacts.

Do not imagine that the person in coma is not aware of what is happening or being said in the room. He is most likely hovering in the energy body over the physical body completely aware of what is going on in the room and how each person is feeling. His consciousness is simply not connected with the physical body and with the conscious mind.

When a person enters this last stage of «acceptance», his room becomes a **shrine filled with spiritual vibrations.** Let us enter it with the respect and joy worthy of such an environment. Let us not fill the air with sorrow, crying, fear and attachment. Our loved one has accepted his departure and we should be happy that he will be experiencing blissful states of consciousness soon. Let us let go of our own fear and attachment and allow these last moments to be filled with peace, love and joy. The dying one will be able thus to leave much more comfortably.

During the stage of acceptance those who are being left behind usually need more help than the one who is departing. Elizabeth Kübler-Ross gives an example of a woman who had faced her death and wanted to be able to die in peace, but was frustrated by her husband's inability to accept the fact that she could actually want to leave him.

First, Elizabeth reports her interview with the woman:
«*She said that the only reason that kept her still alive was her husband's inability to accept the fact that she had to die. She was angry at him for not facing it and for so desperately clinging on to something that she was willing and ready to give up. I translated to her that she wished to detach herself from this world and she nodded gratefully as I left her alone*».

And then the interview with the husband:
«*When I asked him about the patient's needs rather than his own, he sat in silence. He slowly began to realize that he never listened to her needs but took it for granted that they were the same. He could not comprehend that a patient reaches a point when death comes as a great relief, and that patients die easier if they are allowed and helped to detach themselves slowly from all the meaningful relationships in their lives*».

We have another case that comes from Dr. Moody's files concerning an elderly lady close to death:

«*I was with my elderly aunt during her last illness, which was very drawn out. I helped take care of her, and all that time everyone was praying for her to regain her health. She stopped breathing several times. but they brought her back. Finally, one day she looked at me and said, «Jean, I have been over there, over to the beyond, and it is beautiful over there. I want to stay, but I can't as long as you keep praying for me to stay with you. Your prayers are holding me over here. Please don't pray any more! We did all stop, and shortly after that she died*».

Thus we can see that our own attachments can disturb the natural dying process in these last stages, when the individual himself has been able to make peace with the reality of his departure. We must be careful to avoid this if at all possible. Sometimes a complete stranger, who is sensitive and who has experience in facing death with people, can be useful guide during these last moments. He cannot, of course, replace the closest loved ones during these last moments.

He can, however, offer a refreshing, concerned but unattached presence who is familiar with, and unafraid of, the emotions of facing death. I have had the opportunity to play this role a number of times in the past years and it has always been a beautiful and growing experience for me. I always learned much from those beautiful people with whom I shared their last days on earth.

Some of you, who are reading this book, might find yourselves called upon at some time to play this role. You will be able to offer peace, clarity and comfort to the dying one and his loved ones. If you are called upon to play such a role in the future, and the individual involved is able and willing to openly face death, you may find some of the following points useful.

D) HELPING A PERSON TO FACE DEATH CONSCIOUSLY

At the beginning of this chapter we mentioned some general ways in which we can help a dying person regardless of whether he is able to face the reality of his death or not. Summarized, they are:

1) Seeing to his practical needs.

2) Helping him to fulfill his desires and making his environment comfortable.

3) Helping him to learn to relax.

4) Massage, stroking, spiritual healing, therapeutic touch and loving contact.

5) Meditation, prayer and positive projection in which we see him well.

6) To be as cheerful and optimistic as possible (but not falsely so).

If the person is psychologically able to consciously face his impending death and use it as a spiritual growth process, then we can proceed even further.

1) We can discuss any changes or **practical considerations** concerning his last will and testament.

2) We can **discuss with him our beliefs about life and death**. Let him express his beliefs first and express your own only if they are asked for. In discussing your beliefs, you may also refer to some of the reference material that is available concerning what happens after death. (This material has been presented in other chapters). If the dying patient seems to be interested in hearing more, or investigating the subject more deeply, then you may bring him some books or read to him if he is unable to read on his own. You may also bring him recorded lectures or recorded books on such subjects.

A word of caution here. Be sure not to force or push a patient beyond his comfortable limit in facing these matters. As you are speaking, be very sensitive to his facial expressions, in deciding whether to continue or not. If he seems interested and relaxed by the conversation then continue, if not, then change the subject.

It may also be meaningful to discuss views concerning the purpose of life, and why the spirit takes on this physical body. Needless to say such discussions are a spiritual blessing for all involved.

In some cases we may not want to discuss ideas or concepts at all, but simply deal with the emotions we are both feeling. Both he who is dying and he who is being left behind will have a wide range of feelings. It may be a very healing experience for both to communicate deeply their feelings. Also the techniques of "energy psychology" would be very useful here. (See the book *Free to be Happy with Energy Psychology*.)

The most important point is to be totally natural and sincere. Have no preconceived conceptions as you are going into the room of a «dying person» that you are going to discuss «this» or «that». Let everything flow from the heart, but simply **do not be afraid to discuss any issue,** and at the same time, **do not be attached to discussing some particular issue. You are there to serve**, allow the other to guide the flow of the conversation.

3) Another important factor in helping people face death is to help them to **face the various relationship** problems they might have. Help them to discover where they are holding resentment or bitterness towards anyone. Help them to forgive these people and to let go of their negative feelings. If they are unable to let go of these feelings, help them to express them first and then let go of them when they are ready. They might like to write a letter to someone with whom they have some repressed message to express.

If they are unable to face the other person, then they can work on harmonizing the relationship mentally. They can visualize the person and let go of their negative feelings toward that person and send light and love to that person, wishing him to be well. Such an activity is worthwhile whether or not we are facing death. It opens up a whole new flow of life energy and love in us which was blocked by those negative feelings.

4) We can help the dying patient consciously to **let go of this attachments**. This can be done through discussion of their various attachments and the realization that **one really can continue to exist without them.** Often by simply and openly discussing one's fears and attachments, they are gradually surpassed. We can encourage him to concentrate more on the Divine or his *inner immortal self* for this sense of security, thus enabling him to let go of other attachments.

5) Through **guided deep relaxation** and hypnotism the individual can be helped to develop a greater contact with his inner self and with God. He may also be guided into simulated after-death states, in which he experiences himself free from his physical body. Thus he may gradually experience himself as a spiritual being and not simply as a body.

6) He may want to participate in the Christian **sacraments** of Confession and Holy Communion from a clergyman of his religion. If not, he may want to have a confessional type of talk in which he can unload his heart from some of his regrets and doubts.

In general, the individual must be helped to experience himself more as an immortal spiritual being who is about to undergo a transition in focus of consciousness. He needs to increase his contact with his inner self and gradually become free from the attachments and relationships that bind him to the physical world which he must now leave. This process is similar to arranging affairs to move to another country. We must close up our homes and dispose of whatever we cannot take with us. At the same time we will want to have as much information as possible about what to expect in this new place we are going to live in.

How wonderful it would be if in the future, we could all face death with dignity, clarity, peace, joy and spiritual awareness. Hospices have been created in the U.S.A. and Europe where people can spend their last days consciously using them as an opportunity for personal growth and spiritual development. These centers offer a wonderful opportunity both for those who are dying and those who work there.

Perhaps death in the future will be somewhat as Alice Bailey describes it here:

«All I plead is a sane approach to death; all I seek to make is a suggestion that when pain has worn itself out and weakness has supervened, the dying person be permitted to prepare himself, even if apparently unconscious, for the great transition... Is it impossible to conceive of a time when the act of dying will be a triumphant finale to life?

Is it impossible to envision the time when the hours on the deathbed may be but a glorious prelude to a conscious exit? When the fact that the man is to discard the handicap of the physical sheath may be for him and those around him the long-awaited for and joyous consummation? Can you not visualize the time when, instead of tears and fears and refusal to recognize the inevitable, the dying person and his friends would mutually agree on the hour, and that nothing but happiness would characterize the passing?... I tell you that before so very long, this will be deeply so for the intelligent of the race and little by little for all».

E) GUIDING THE SPIRIT ONCE IT HAS LEFT THE PHYSICAL BODY

We have mentioned in the earlier chapters that the spirit is able to hear and see what is going on here on this earthly plane, even after its departure from the physical body. We have also mentioned that the spirit may be a little disorientated during the first days as it has to reorient itself to a new set of laws and conditions which it finds in the after-death state.

There will, of course, be spirit guides who will help the spirit in this process of transition. We can also help out by communicating certain guidance to the spirit during the various stages of his after-death existence.

The rate at which the spirit will pass through the various after-death existences will vary from spirit to spirit. Also, the experiences he will have will vary according to the contents of the mind that he has taken with him upon leaving the body.

Here are some general guidelines which we can follow concerning our communication with the spirits in those moments after death. The following information is taken from the **Tibetan Book of the Dead.**

THE FIRST 20 MINUTES TO 4 HOURS

The first moments after the spirit leaves the physical body represent a great opportunity for it to evolve spiritually, if it is able to keep his mind positively oriented.

For the **first twenty minutes** it is considered that the spirit will be facing a **pure light**, which is so overpoweringly brilliant, that the spirit avoids looking directly at it. During these moments the spirit can be guided verbally or non-verbally not to fear the White

Light and to face it and merge with it. This Pure Light can be considered to be the *Christ Light* in Christian terms. Many of Moody's cases saw this brilliant light and were amazed by it. **The individual should be encouraged to merge with it**.

After the first twenty minutes the individual can be guided in three ways according to his nature and state of evolution:

1) If he was a person who has done much meditation and had worked on controlling the mind, we explain to him that whatever he is seeing is simply a reflection of his own pure consciousness. The Pure White Light is in reality his own pure consciousness – he should merge with it.

2) If the person was religious and worshiped a particular form of God, then we can guide him to see that form before him now and feel the blessing of that divine being. We can then guide him to merge with his chosen deity.

3) If the person has no particular deity which he worshiped, then he can be guided to meditate on the "Great Compassionate Lord" in whatever way that he can. He is guided to bring to his mind some concept of *God*, however God may appear for that spirit.

AFTER 4 HOURS AND FOR THE
NEXT THREE TO FOUR DAYS

After 4 hours the opportunity of using the Pure White Light for liberation has passed and if the spirit has not succeeded (something which we cannot really know), it will go on to other experiences. In the case of the advanced spirits, we should remind it over and over that whatever it is experiencing is simply the contents of its mind – that what it is seeing is its own thought forms taking shape before it. We encourage the spirit to have no fear of anything that it sees and neither to be attracted to anything that it may see, but rather to simply watch it all like a movie.

Those who have had religious inclinations during their earth years are encouraged to concentrate on, and pray to their deity. We may even imagine the departed spirit to be in the presence and protection of God.

For those who have had no spiritual inclinations we can encourage them to listen to the advice of the spirit guides who have come to help them with the transition.

AS THE DAYS PASS

There is no time – in the dimension in which the spirit now exists – and thus it is difficult to talk about the beginning and ending of these after-death stages. An advanced spirit may immediately leave the earth plane and need no guidance at all. Another spirit, who was very attached to the earth plane, may hang around for years and need much guidance and advice from both dimensions in order to let go and continue with his evolution.

There is some general advice that can be given to spirits, however, after the fourth day. We can communicate the following to them verbally or mentally.

1) Death comes to all; it is nothing unusual. It is a perfectly normal state.

2) There is no sense in clinging to earthly life out of attachment or weakness.

3) You have no power to remain, even if you want to.

4) If you try to remain, you will just get lost in endless, futile searching.

5) Remember and focus on God.

6) Do not fear anything that you see.

7) All that you see are reflections of your own mind.

8) Those images you see are simply the nature of the experience you are passing through. They are not permanent; they will not last. (Regardless of whether they are pleasant or unpleasant).

9) Do not be afraid of any strong lights or sounds. They are simply the creations of your own mind;
just observe them.

10) Since you now exist in your thought-body and do not have a physical body, you are incapable of being harmed or dying.

11) Do not be disturbed by anything that is happening here on the earth. Be detached from everything and feel only love for all beings.

12) Use your ability to pray and meditate in your new environment and concentrate to God and Love.

We may visualize our loved one flowing upward surrounded by, and/or on a ray of light in the guidance of angels moving towards God and continuing with his spiritual evolution.

And then, in order that the spirit may freely ascend, we must let go of our attachment to it and our sorrow, and learn to live in joy and love.

CHAPTER IV.

THE REINCARNATION
OF SAADA HATOUM

By Jumana Juwayri,
Reprinted from the Beirut, Lebanon magazine
Monday Morning April 1978

FIVE-YEAR-OLD SUZY CHANEM INSISTS THAT SHE IS THE MOTHER OF THREE ADULT CHILDREN, AND HER «CHILDREN» ARE CONVINCED THAT SHE IS.

AN INTIMATE LOOK AT THE STRANGEST SET OF FAMILY RELATIONSHIPS IN LEBANON TODAY.

Saada Hatoum died in the United States on April 11, 1972.
Suzanne Chanem was born in Lebanon on April 21, 1972.
Suzanne Chanem is now five years old.
She insists that she is not Suzanne Chanem.
She tells her parents that she is Saada Hatoum, that she died after surgery in the United States and that she wants her children and husband back.
The Ghanems and the Hatoums had never heard of each other before. Suzanne (Saada?), however, sought out her children and contacted them, and her children - all adults - are now convinced that their mother is a five-year-old girl who lives in Shwaifat, a southern suburb of Beirut.
Saada's daughter, Ghada, wife of Fuad Halabi, told me:
«My mother has been reincarnated in a little girl. I am sure of it. She talks and acts like my mother. She tells us things about ourselves that she could never have known if she had been anyone other than my mother. She talks about our intimate secrets. She knows all our relatives. She has the soul of my mother».

VISITING SUZY

Ghada's husband is equally convinced, and so are the parents of the little girl, and no one is more supremely confident than the girl herself, as I found out when I visited her.

Would she be a little tyke with adult manners? I half expected that. I was wrong. She was a typical child - shy, and suspicious of strangers, including me.

For a while, she refused to answer my questions. Then Ghada interfered.

«Answer her questions, Saada», she said. «She 's my friend. You can tell her».

Suzy leaned over and said in a whisper which could be heard around the room: «You (Ghada) are my daughter, just as Leila is my daughter and Walid is my son. I hope you will have a son».

I ventured another question: «But how can you be Ghada's mother when you are so much younger?»

«I 'm talking about when I was in the past generation», she informed me.

FIRST NAMES

Backtracking a few years, I asked Suzy's father, Shaheen Ghanem, when his daughter started conjuring up the past.

The first names she ever mentioned, he told me, were Leila (Saada Hatoum's daughter, wife of the Lebanese consul in Venezuela) and Walid (her grandson and Leila's son).

«She kept repeating them over and over again. She was only two years old then. We couldn't ask her who these people were. Then she added other names: Melhem (Saada's husband), Ghada and Nabil (her other two children), Aristotle, Plato, Pitagore, Fares and Mazed (her brothers).

«She did not mention any family names, so we had no way of knowing what she was talking about. But we knew she must be the reincarnation of someone, and we tried to help her remember».

The breakthrough, Shaheen Ghanem said, came entirely by accident.

«We had visitors, and we were talking about a person named Noura. Suzy jumped up as soon as she heard the name. «Noura»,

she said, «is the wife of my brother Mazed. He died before me».
That is how we found out. Mazed is the MEA pilot who died in the
1963 crash in Abu Dhabi. His wife was Noura. After that, we were
able to help Suzanne remember more. The older she got, the more
details she would tell us about her past life - her husband, her
children, her brothers».
During the 1975-76 war, Suzy became hysterical.
«She often cried, shouting for her children», Shaheen said. «She
was a mother, and she was worried about her daughter and her son.
She wrote us the telephone number of her previous home. It was
correct with one inversion: a 68 was written 86.

«I'M YOUR MOTHER»

The Hatoums first heard of their reincarnated mother through a
letter to Leila Esrawi Hatoum, in Venezuela. Suzy had remembered
her «daughter's» old address and written to her. Since Leila's
husband, being a consul, was well-known, the letter, with Suzy's
photo, followed Leila to her new address.
It read something like this:
«I am your mother. Write to me. My name now is Suzanne
Ghanem. I live in Shwaifat».
Leila, not knowing what to make of this, wrote to her sister and
father in Beirut asking them to look into the matter. The Hatoums
- Melhem and his children Ghada and Nabil - went to Shwaifat the
day after they received Leila's letter.
When Suzy saw them, she froze. She could not move or speak for a
while.
Melhem, looking at the frightened girl, had his doubts. A hoax, he
thought to himself, someone's out for money.
But Suzy soon calmed down and started to talk. She spoke freely of
Hatoum family's affairs, and she mentioned one major fact which,
as far as the Hatoums were concerned, was the clincher.
Turning to Ghada, the little girl asked: «Did your uncle Aristo give
you your jewels? Did he give Leila hers?»
The Hatoums were convinced. Only three people, they told me,
knew about the jewels. Saada gave them to her brother Aristotle in
the United States just before she died, with instructions that he
distribute them between her daughters Leila and Ghada.

The more Suzy spoke, the more convinced the Hatoums became. The strange relationship between the child mother/wife and her family had begun.

CHILD WIFE

Suzy refers to Melhem as her husband. When she visits him, she sits in his lap and leans her head on his chest. At one point, she got word that he had married again. She was very upset and she called him immediately:

«Did you really get married», she asked, «or is it just a rumor?»
«What do you think?» he said.
«I don't think you did, because I'm the only girl in your life», she answered.

He did not have the heart to tell her the truth – that he had indeed married again. When she visits him and sees his wife, she considers her «the neighbor».

Ghada lives in Saudi Arabia these days, but she often comes to Beirut. When she's in town, she receives at least two calls a day from her «mother», who often chides her for neglecting to call.

«Instead of you calling your mother, you wait 'til she calls you», she says sternly. «Are you taking care of yourself? You are pregnant, and you must be very careful. Don't exert yourself. I think you're going to have a baby boy. Leila should have a baby girl, since she already has a son... When you go back to Riyadh, tell my mother (Zahra, who is also living in Saudi Arabia) not to forget to write to me. Tell Aristo and Socrates the same thing».

CHANGES

Ghada remembers that when Suzy first visited Melhem Hatoum's home, she immediately noticed that things were different. «I see you've changed things around since I left», she said. «Especially in the bedrooms».

Suzy was shown the Hatoum's photo albums. She picked out all the relatives and named them accurately:

«This is my brother Aristo, my brother Socrates, my brother Pitagore, my mother... and this is me. I think I'm wearing my black dress here. I recognize the cut. Look how thin I was». She paused, and the memory of pain was obvious in her eyes. «I was very sick». Saada Hatoum, in fact, suffered from heart trouble for a long time before it was decided to send her to the U.S. for surgery. The operation was dangerous, and it proved fatal. On her way to the U.S. she stopped in Venezuela and visited her daughter Leila and her grandson Walid. Leila was supposed to follow her to the U.S. She was delayed, and Saada died asking for her. Perhaps, the Hatoums speculate, that is why the first names Suzy uttered were Leila and Walid.

Trying to describe her feeling toward her infant mother, Ghada Hatoum Halabi told me: «I love her soul, and I am attracted by her personality. She's as sweet as my mother was. She has the same eyes, although my mother's were blue, and many of my mother's traits. Knowing Suzy has helped me. I have learned from her that my mother did not suffer when she died. Having her here is a comfort. I don't cry over my mother, as I often used to do».

«WE BELIEVE»

Suzy's father, Shaheen, says both he and his wife cherish their child «in a special way».

«We believe in what is happening to her», he said.

The child's attitude toward her parents is a mixture of rejection and acceptance. When the memories press in on her, she rebels: «You are not my parents», she says, «and my name is not Suzy. I am Saada. My house is much larger and prettier than this».

But then she says to her father: «I love you. You are kind to me, as my father Asaad used to be. That is why I accept you».

And she chatters amiably with her mother, often telling her that she would help her around the house. «I must give you some of my cake recipes», she said once. «I'm very good at baking cakes».

But the Hatoums and the Ghanems see a profound sadness in Suzy and they pity her.

«She is a child, with a child's feeling, but she worries about her children and is saddened by her separation from them», her father told me. «She often cries when she thinks of them. She hasn't seen Leila yet, because Leila is in Venezuela, and she rarely sees Ghada, who is in Saudi Arabia most of the time. She calls Melhem Hatoum's home daily, and she says: «Let me talk to my husband».

I have often heard her ask him: «Do you still love me? I love you. You were very good to me».

Ghada senses Suzy's sorrow. «I know how much she is suffering, and I know her suffering will grow with her», she says.

When I saw Suzy, I saw a shy little girl. When I heard her, I heard a mother.

They played a tape for me that Suzy had recorded to send to her mother, brothers and daughter in Saudi Arabia.

«When you come to see me», she said quietly, «I don't want any of you to be wearing black».

And when I left the Ghanem residence, I looked back at the girl who was staring out at me through the window. Her brown eyes were filled with tears.

ANCIENT BELIEF

Is Suzanne Ghanem Saada Hatoum reincarnate?

Sheik Mohammed Khalil Al-Bacha, a prominent Druze author and the president of the Lebanese National Lottery, would not be surprised if she were.

He, like all the Druze community, has no doubt that reincarnation is a fact.

«Reincarnation», he told me, «is the theory which holds that the soul moves from one body to another after death and rises in the spiritual scale through the experiences it encounters in lifetime after lifetime within the context of one everlasting life which starts and ends with God».

The theory, he said, is an ancient one, and was included in the original secret Indian creed. «It was later advocated by Pythagoras, Plato and others, and it is the theory through which we interpret the Koranic verse: «How disbelieve ye in Allah when ye were dead and he gave life to you! Then he will give you death, then life again, and then unto Him ye will return». (The Cow, 28)».

ANSWERS

Reason, Sheik Mohammed argued, dictates the adoption of the reincarnation theory for the explanation of such matters as the following:

«**First**: If the soul is eternal, as indeed it is, where was it before its birth? Things eternal must spring from eternity, and if the soul sprang from nothingness, then it is not eternal, for the ultimate end of nothingness is nothingness, and that is not the case with the soul. The theory of reincarnation answers this question as follows: Since the soul is eternal, it must have had a past before birth and it must have a future after death.

«**Second**: What wrong have those who are born blind or deformed done? Is it true that the sins of the fathers are visited upon the sons? Does this not conflict with the concept of divine justice? The deformities with which some are born, however, can be explained through the reincarnation theory as the wages of sins committed in past lives.

«**Third**: Why is it that some who are known to be good people are plagued by misfortune, while many of those who deserve misfortune are blessed with plenty? Far be it from the Almighty to be lacking in justice. The good people who are beset by trials and tribulations, if viewed through the reincarnation theory, are being tested and purged, as gold is purified by fire.
The Koran says: «And surely We shall try you with something of fear and hunger and loss of wealth and lives and crops; but give glad tidings to the steadfast, who say when a misfortune striketh them: Lo we are Allah's and lo! unto him we are returning». (The Cow, 155, 156).
Likewise, the good fortune which is granted to those who apparently do not deserve it is a test which either helps them to advance or leads them into crooked paths, for which they will be held to account, either in this life or in future lives.

«**Fourth**: How would you explain the disparity in character and intelligence between children born to the same parents and raised in identical environments? The difference, according to the theory of reincarnation, lies in the number of reincarnations each child has gone through and the extent to which the child has benefited from each».

«UTTERANCE»

Evidence of reincarnation, Sheik Mohammed noted, can be seen in the ability of hypnosis to carry their subjects' minds back to past lives - lives which the subjects have on several occasions described with uncanny detail.

Further evidence, he added, is provided by cases like that of Suzanne Ghanem.

«This is what we call "utterance". It occurs when the mind retains memories of a past life. This has happened often, and it has repeatedly been proven that the "utterance" is neither a hoax nor an instance of paramnesia. It has apparently happened in the case which you are investigating».

Why, I asked him, does "utterance" occur only in a few cases, if it is true that all living souls have had past lives?

«Spiritual teachings say that the immense mind of man cannot possibly be contained in the limited form of the human body. A man's mind cannot manifest itself fully in one incarnation. Part of it is manifested, the rest remains dormant. The dormant part of the mind is what psychologists call the subconscious. That is why remembrance of lives past is so rare. It is only after death that the full mind of man comes together and becomes whole».

«Utterance», he said, «is the words used to describe the rare cases when a child remembers and speaks about a past life».

Children who «utter» are usually ignored or discouraged by their elders, unless they happen to belong to the Druze community - as the Hatoums and the Ghanems do - which tends to encourage the children to remember more.

FADING MEMORIES

Memories of past incarnations will stay with a child longer if that child finds encouragement from his elders, but regardless of the elders' reactions, the memories will eventually fade to be overshadowed by the new experiences which the child goes through as he grows older.

Sheik Mohammed, asked about the emotional crises which Suzy appears to be going through as a result of her memories, told me: «These are brought on by purely materialistic links which linger in the mind despite death and rebirth. The child is unaware of the materialistic nature of those past ties, and the emotional suffering which the memories cause exhaust her. But this will not last long. When other experiences intervene and other ties are firmly formed, the memories, should they linger, will elicit little emotional response».

The divine rationale behind reincarnation Sheik Mohammed explained as follows: «Man has never been able, nor will he ever be able, to fathom the divine will, but the Almighty has given our minds enough understanding to speculate on this matter. We say that the purpose of Man's existence on earth cannot possibly be fulfilled in one brief lifetime. Of what value is a lifetime, no matter how long it may seem by our standards, to the progress of an eternal soul? The experiences the soul needs to gain awareness and self-knowledge cannot possibly be contained in limited time or space».

HEAVEN AND HELL

The reincarnation theory, Sheik Mohammed told us does not negate the concepts of heaven and hell. «On the contrary, it gives it a rational explanation which promotes faith on the basis of full awareness».

He explained:

«As I have said, the divine essence of Man uses the body in a succession of lives to effect spiritual progress and, by completing that progress mentally and morally, to attain eternal happiness. The more progress man achieves, the more he will enjoy his freedom of will. The freedom of will teaches him to bear the responsibility of his unrestricted action - and that is the basic principle behind the concepts of crime and punishment. The Koran says: «Who so doth right, he is for his soul, and who so doth wrong, it is against it. And afterward unto your Lord ye will be brought back». (Crouching, ا4).

«Thus, good deeds become a source of joy for the doer, and bad deeds a source of sorrow and suffering. Joy is the paradise of the heart, and sorrow is the fire and brimstone of the heart. Man's judge is his conscience, and the conscience is a merciless judge who often drives man to take his own life.

After death, man sees his good and bad deeds piled up before him, and his conscience, much more powerful after its release from the corporal shell, metes out the reward and the punishment. Then comes reincarnation and return to the body, and Man, his memories of what happened before erased, is given another chance to progress.

«Man, in other words, carries his paradise and his hell in his conscience, which holds him to account at the end of every incarnation, until he achieves spiritual supremacy and enjoys the happiness which this achievement will give him.

«When the final day comes - «When the Earth is shaken with a shock and the hills are ground to powder» (The Event, 4,5,6), when our planet, like so many others, dies and is buried in the great cemetery of space - there will be those who will have achieved their happiness long before and are no longer in need of a return to Earth; there will be those whose reincarnations and their little hells have succeeded in holding them, and these too will have no more need to return; but they will be lost forever in the Hades of their past deeds.

The Holy Koran explains this clearly: «And ye will be three kinds: those on the right hand... and those on the left hand... and the foremost in the race. The foremost in the race, those are they who will be brought nigh, in gardens of delight... And those on the right hand among thornless date-trees, and clustered plantations and spreading shade... And those on the left hand in scorching wind and scalding water and shadow of black smoke».

Suzy Ghanem remembers her last visit to earth, the Sheik said, but she will forget, as we have forgotten, and she, like us, will continue her progress, through reincarnation after reincarnation, toward spreading shade or the shadow of black smoke.

CHAPTER V

SOME INTERESTING QUOTATIONS ABOUT REINCARNATION

Most people are unaware how many deeply respected thinkers of the western world accepted the concept of reincarnation. Here are just a few quotations which you will probably find interesting and even surprising.

JESUS OF NAZARETH: «Whom do men say that I the Son of man am?» And the disciples answered: «Some say that thou art Elijah, and others Jeremiah, or one of the prophets». «Verily I say unto you, Among them that are born of women there hath not risen a greater than John the Baptist. And if you will receive it, this is Elijah who was destined to come. He that hath ears to hear, let him hear».
Matthew 16:13-14, 11:11, 14-15.

PLATO: O youth or young man, who fancy that you are neglected by the Gods, know that if you become worse you shall go to the worse souls, or if better to the better, and in every succession of life and death you will do and suffer what like may fitly suffer at the hand of like. This is the justice of heaven, which neither you nor any other unfortunate will ever glory in escaping. Take heed thereof, for it will be sure to take heed of you. If you say – I am small and will creep into the depths of the earth, or I am high and will fly up to heaven, you are not so small or so high that you shall not pay the fitting penalty. And thinkest thou, bold man, that thou neediest not to know this? – he who knows it not can never form any true idea of the happiness or unhappiness of life or hold any rational discourse respecting either.
Laws (Book X)

HERMES TRISMEGISTUS: The Soul passes from form to form; and the mansions of her pilgrimage are manifold. Thou puttest off thy bodies as raiment, and as vesture dost thou fold them up. Thou art from old, O Soul of man, yea, thou art from everlasting.
Egyptian Hermetic Fragments

ALBERT SCHWEITZER: By reason of the idea of reincarnation Indian thought can be reconciled to the fact that so many people in their minds and actions are still so engrossed in the world. If we assume that we have but one existence, there arises the insoluble problem of what becomes of the spiritual ego which has lost all contact with the Eternal. Those who hold the doctrine of reincarnation are faced by no such problem. For them that non-spiritual attitude only means that those men and women have not yet attained to the purified form of existence in which they are capable of knowing the truth and translating it into action. So the idea of reincarnation contains a most comforting explanation of reality by means of which Indian thought surmounts difficulties which baffle the thinkers of Europe.
Indian Thought and Its Development

BENJAMIN FRANKLIN: Finding myself to exist in the world, I believe I shall in some shape or other always exist, and with all the inconvenience human life is liable to, I shall not object to a new edition of mine, hoping, however, that the errata of the last may be corrected.
Letters

GOETHE: I am certain that I have been here as I am now a thousand times before, and I hope to return a thousand times. When one reflects upon the eternity of the universe, one can conceive of no other destiny than that the Monads or Souls should eventually participate in the bliss of the Gods as joyfully cooperating forces. The work of creation will be entrusted to them. Man is the dialogue between nature and God. On other planets this dialogue will doubtless be of a higher and profounder character.
Conversation with Johannes Falk

CARL JUNG: My life as I lived it had often seemed to me like a story that has no beginning and no end. I had the feeling that I was a historical fragment, an expert for which the preceding and succeeding text was missing. I could well imagine that I might have lived in former centuries and there encountered questions I was not yet able to answer that I had to be born again because I had not fulfilled the task that was given to me. When I die, my deeds will flow along with me – that is how I imagine it. I will bring with me what I have done. In the meantime it is important to insure that I do not stand at the end with empty hands.
Memories, Dreams, Reflections

TOLSTOY: How interesting it would be to write the story of the experiences in this life of a man who killed himself in his previous life; how he now stumbles against the very demands which had offered themselves before, until he arrives at the realization that he must fulfill those demands... The deeds of the preceding life give direction to the present life. This is what the Hindus call Karma.
Diary and other writings

NIETZSCHE: My doctrine is: Live so that thou mayest desire to live again – that is my duty – for in any case thou wilt live again! This doctrine is lenient towards those who do not believe in it. It speaks of no hells and it contains no threats. He who does not believe in it has but a fleeting life in his consciousness. Let us guard against teaching such a doctrine as if it were a suddenly discovered religion! It must percolate through slowly, and whole generations must build on it and become fruitful through it – in order that it may grow into a large tree which will shelter all posterity.
Eternal Recurrence

GIORDANO BRUNO: I have held and hold souls to be immortal. Speaking as a Catholic, they do not pass from body to body, but go to Paradise, Purgatory, or Hell. But I have reasoned deeply, and, speaking as a philosopher, since the soul is not found without body and yet is not body, it may be in one body or in another, and pass from body to body. From Spirit, the Life of the Universe, proceeds the life and soul of everything that has soul and life.
Bruno's Trial before the Inquisition

BALZAC: Who knows how many fleshly forms the heir of heaven occupies before he can be brought to understand the value of that silence and solitude whose starry plains are but the vestibule of Spiritual Worlds? A lifetime may be needed merely to gain the virtues which annul the errors of man's preceding life. The virtues we acquire, which develop slowly within us, are the invisible links that bind each one of our existences to the others – existences which the spirit alone remembers, for Matter has no memory for spiritual things. The endless legacy of the past to the present is the secret source of human genius.
Seraphita

THOMAS HUXLEY: In the doctrine of transmigration, whatever its origin, Brahmanical and Buddhist speculation found, ready to hand, the means of constructing a plausible vindication of the ways of the Cosmos to man. None but very hasty thinkers will reject it on the ground of inherent absurdity. Like the doctrine of evolution itself, that of transmigration has its roots in the world of reality.
Evolution and Ethics

HENRIK IBSEN: There is One who ever reappears, at certain intervals, in the course of human history. He is like a rider taming a wild horse in the arena. Again and yet again it throws him. A moment, and he is in the saddle again, each time more secure and more expert; but off he has had to go, in all his varying incarnations, until this day. Who knows how often he has wandered among us when none have recognized him?
The Emperor Julian

Our so-called individual existence is in reality nothing but a mere process of these "bodily and mental" phenomena, which since immemorial times was going on before one's apparent birth, and which also after death will continue for immemorial periods of time.
Buddha, the Word (The Eightfold Path)

CHAPTER VI

WHY I BELIEVE IN REINCARNATION

I used to be an Atheist, or perhaps an Agnostic would be a better term. I believed we had probably created the idea of God, in order to calm our fears and insecurities about life. I did not believe in reincarnation, Karma, evolution, God or any other spiritual concepts. I was a chemical engineer who believed only in the physical facts which could be proved with objective scientific experiments.

This lack of belief in anything caused me to lose my interest in life. I saw no reason for living or doing right or wrong. I passed through a crisis in which life had no meaning for me. When this crisis became intense enough, I decided that I could not continue life in this way, and that I would have to search deeply into the purpose and explanations of life in order to continue. I decided that life without meaning or purpose was not worth living.

So I left my job as a chemical engineer and began searching for some answers. I wanted to know the answers to some basic questions, such as:
What am I?
Who am I?
What am I doing here on earth?
Where was I before I came to this earth?
Where will I go when I leave here?
What exactly am I supposed to do while I am here?
What is the purpose of human life?
What is God, if He (She)exits?
What is His/Her nature?

How did all this come into existence &
Who is asking all these questions?

It was only many years later that I discovered that many others in
history were concerned about these questions – Socrates, Plato,
Pythagoras, as well as most of the great philosophical and religious
leaders of the world.

My search began, and had continued for 15 years until the writing
this book. I do not think it will ever end, because reality is
somewhat like an onion with an infinite number of layers to be
uncovered. Every time we remove another veil of ignorance to see
the truth a little more clearly, we discover that there is yet another
veil and another and another to be removed.

For this reason, I am cautious not to be dogmatic about what I
believe, for I see that even in a scientific understanding of the
world, our view of reality is constantly changing. That which was
scientifically true some years ago, is no longer considered the truth,
as we dig deeper into the nature of the physical world. How much
truer this must be of our metaphysical understanding. Thus I allow
my belief system to be flexible enough to grow with the new
information which comes into my consciousness.

Now I believe in the concept of reincarnation, Karma and the
evolution of the soul as the best explanations of our existence here
on the earth which I have heard as of yet. That means that these are
to me the most logical explanations, which explain more questions
about life than any other concepts which I have heard until now. In
the future, if I should come in contact with a better explanation,
then I will gladly accept it.

Many people have asked me why I believe in reincarnation. In the
following pages I will try to explain some of the reasons and
experiences which have contributed to my belief in reincarnation of
the soul through various lifetimes as it learns more and more about
life and about its own nature.

The idea is that the spirit, for some reason, has separated from its perfect eternal state of union with God and is experiencing life in the physical world. Although the Spirit, in reality, remains perfect in its union with God, its projection on the earth plane, that is, the soul in the incarnated body, loses its awareness of that divine state. The soul then begins to experience and experiment with the physical world by entering into physical vehicles.

At first the soul could manifest itself only through very simple vehicles such as one-celled organisms like amoebas. Eventually as the soul has more and more contact with the physical world, through repeated birth and death of these various simple forms of life, it gradually develops the ability to incarnate into more advanced physical vehicles, such as plants, fish, insects, animals, primates and finally human beings.

This fits in very well with the Darwinian theory of the evolution of the species and a new theory of evolution by a modern biologist Rupert Sheldrake. From this point of view we see that evolution is taking place in the vehicle through which the soul is expressing itself here on the earth. Sheldrake's theory is similar to the eastern concept of a causal or spiritual body, which he calls the morphogenetic field. The concept is that the evolution of the species both in terms of physical structure and behavior is the result of the evolution of a subtle energy field which gives shape to and guides the functioning of the various living beings. We may call this the *morphogenetic field*, the *causal body* or the *soul*.

This evolution takes place as the soul learns through trial and error to adapt itself to earth conditions, and expands its freedom and capacity of expression here on the earth. Now evolution continues in mental, psychic and spiritual realms. Theoretically we are all evolving towards becoming super humans, saints or angels. So we reincarnate again and again, perfecting ourselves a little more each time we come, sometimes moving forward and sometimes falling backwards. Some souls seem to learn more quickly.

The concept of reincarnation and Karma will become clearer as we discuss them further in the text. Now let me begin to explain some of the reasons why I have come to believe in Reincarnation.

BOOKS THAT I READ

During the first years of searching, I read a number of books about eastern philosophy, religion, psychology, education, science and any other subject which I thought would help me understand myself and the world more clearly. Certainly books are not authorities. If we examine what we know, however, we will find that a very high percentage of it is from books. The convincing point was this – that all the books I was reading were saying the same thing.

Whether I was reading eastern mystics, nuclear physicists, humanistic psychologists, or modern mediumistic communications, they all gave the following very clear message: The human being is comprised of an eternal soul nature and a physical-mental instrument through which the soul functions on the earth. The physical-mental vehicle is temporary and dies in each successive life, but the soul, along with its tendencies developed in the previous lives, continues from incarnation to incarnation. The purpose of this series of incarnations is for the soul to learn to express its own loving, creative and blissful nature through the body and mind right here on this earth. This takes thousands of lifetimes of lessons, and each experience within each lifetime is an opportunity to learn and evolve, if the proper attitude is taken.

This «Perennial philosophy» as it is called by Aldous Huxley who fully embraced it, is supported by the eastern religions of Buddhism, Hinduism, Taoism, Ancient Greek philosophy, and esoteric ancient Egyptian, Sufi and even esoteric Christian teachings. In addition, today it is being verified by many books, and is being communicated to us by souls from «the other side». That is, by souls who have completed their incarnations and are able to use the minds of certain individuals here on the earth to communicate the details of the death process, life between lives, the laws which govern reincarnation, as well as the birth process.

One of the many books which I found very useful was **Many Mansions** by Gina Cerminara. She compiled data from the 2,500 life readings given by psychic Edgar Cayce from 1923 to 1945.

During these life readings, Cayce went into hypnotic trances and his mind connected to the universal mind, called the «Akashic Records», and gave forth information concerning the individual's physical, emotional, mental and spiritual state.

In most cases, there was an illness involved and the people wanted cures. Cures were suggested, and when applied they worked. But to the everyone's surprise, including Cayce himself who was a devout Christian and read **The Bible** cover to cover every year of his adult life, the readings also began to mention the cause of disease and sufferings as having the origin in past lives. At first Cayce didn't want to believe it. But the «Source» was always correct about the most minute details of people's lives, and it so often referred to the teachings of Christ, that he eventually had to accept the reality of Reincarnation and Karma.

Many answers to the enigmas of life came out of these «Life readings». Answers to questions I never expected to find answers to. And as I studied further, I saw that these answers were in complete harmony with many other sources, such as **Seth Speaks,** by Jane Roberts, all the Alice Bailey books and the teachings of those philosophies already mentioned above. Let us look at some of those answers.

THE CONCEPT OF REINCARNATION
EXPLAINS MANY QUESTIONS ABOUT LIFE

a) One question which must enter every person's mind is, **«why do some people suffer more than others?** Especially new born children?»

If I accept the concept of a **"just God"**, then why should He give more to one and less to another? Why should a child be born crippled, blind or handicapped in any way? Why should some children suffer the cruelty of ignorant parents, and others be given such loving care? **Why?**

Reincarnation supplies a reasonable answer, as expressed by the Source in one of the Cayce readings. «*This suffering is Karma for both the parent and the child*. Karma is a law of the universe which ensures that every thought, word and deed expressed by a human being must come back to him. This is the basis of the teachings of all great teachers. *«As you sow, so shall you reap»*.

So the condition of every newborn child is dictated by his or her thoughts, words and deeds in previous incarnations. This is hinted in the disciples' question to Christ about whether the man blind from birth was that way as a result of his own sins or those of his parents.

How could a man be born blind, as a result of his own sins unless he had had a previous life in which to sin? As the Cayce reading indicates, the karma is usually for both the child and the parents who will have to care for it.

Number of lives

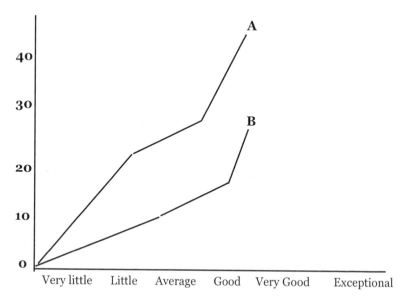

Degree of perfection of specific Talent or ability

b) At the same time, some children are born with a **genius** for various talents, such as Chopin or Mozart for music. There was no way they could have developed those abilities in the lives in which they excelled. By the reincarnation principle, we can assume that souls can develop talents from life to life. Children and adults with special inclinations and talents have been developing them for thousands of years through hundreds of lives. Many of us have many hidden talents which we have not yet uncovered in this life.

Consider the model above. Notice the soul «**A**» has spent more energy and time developing this particular trait or talent over the lifetimes than soul «**B**». Soul «B» may have been developing along other lines. So that when «A» and «B» are born into their 30th lifetime, «A» may have an advanced talent for music, while «B» will be less musically inclined but perhaps more oriented toward engineering. Thus we may explain the innate talent which each person has toward specific activities or creative arts. We seem to know how to do many things without actually learning them in this life.

c) Children born with basically the same hereditary and environmental conditions (including identical twins) develop very **different personalities** with different interests and sensitivities. This is because each child brings with it into the new body a «conditioning» based on previous life experiences. Just as we understand a child is conditioned by its early childhood experiences, it is also conditioned by its previous life experiences. In fact, a soul will often **choose** family and environmental surroundings which will recreate past life conditions so that it can pick up where it left off.

Seth, who speaks through Jane Roberts from the «other side» expresses it in this way:

«In each life you choose and create your own settings or environments; and in this one you chose your parents and whatever childhood incidents that came within your experience. You wrote the script».

d) Many **psychological problems** and traits can be explained as the results of past life experiences. For example, the Cayce readings have found the cause of an irrational fear of water in one woman to be a result of a subconscious memory of drowning to death in a previous life. Another woman, totally paranoid about having children, was told that she had seen six children die in a fire in a lifetime in 17th Century France. Another subject who came with a problem of extreme claustrophobia, to the point of being unable to ride in a crowded bus, or go to the movie theater, was released from the fear when it was pointed out that it was the subconscious memory of a previous death in a collapsed cave.

Therapy is being done today by psychologists with techniques of hypnotic regression into past lives. Authoress Joan Grant and her psychiatrist husband Denys Kelsey have helped many people by guiding them to re-experience traumatic events of the past lives so as to release these memories from their subconscious hiding places.

One dramatic cure came to a woman who was unreasonably afraid of feathers and birds. In a past life regression she experienced her self as a male soldier in an ancient Persian lifetime in which she/he died on the battlefield. Before she was unconscious, however, the vultures came and started eating her (or his) flesh. This subconscious memory was the basis of the unexplainable fear of feathers. After the regression she lost the fear.

e) Other types of psychological and physical suffering can also be traced to previous life causes. Epilepsy in many cases is the result of a misuse of sexual energy or psychic ability in past lives. The apparent injustice of the infidelity of a mate is often the result of the so-called «innocent one» having done the same in a previous existence.

Of course not all karma is unpleasant. Good deeds bring pleasant results. One reason why so much of the material reflects unpleasant karma, is that people go for life readings and question their life only when there are problems or suffering. This is natural, in the sense that our natural state should be one of health and happiness. If we do not have that, then something is going wrong and we should try to discover what it is and correct it. The purpose of karma is to help us see where we are going so that we can adjust the way we think and act.

A case of goodness returning is that of a New York model who had such beautiful hands that they were extremely popular and gave her financial support. The Cayce reading gave the reason

«The Karmic cause for her gift of beauty was found in the incarnation immediately preceding the present, when she was a recluse in an English convent. Her life had been spent in performing menial and distasteful tasks with her hands; she did them with such a dedicated spirit of selflessness and service, however, that her consecration of spirit was transmuted into the unusual beauty of her person and her hands».

Perhaps this sheds some light on Jesus' «Sermon on the Mount», in which he says the meek shall inherit the earth. We surely don't see them inheriting the earth in their present lifetime. And He didn't say that they would inherit Heaven. He said the Earth. Perhaps he was indicating that those who practiced humility would find their rewards in the next life.

f) The preference of **Homosexuality** can perhaps be explained by the reincarnation theory. Cayce and Seth agree that male homosexuals are souls who have taken a male body after many consecutive lives in female bodies. These souls, may have felt that they were getting a bit polarized in their development and chose to swing back towards the center of the male - female polarity by taking a male body in order to develop male tendencies.

For some of them, however, the female characteristics are so overdeveloped that an inner struggle takes place between the previous conditioning and the type of body taken. The soul's purpose is to become balanced in its expression.

The soul has no sex. Sex is only attributed to the body and to mental characteristics. In-between lives there is no sex, but a soul may have developed itself in one sexual role more than another.

In the same way the conflict which Lesbians feel is the result of a soul taking a female body, after a series of male lives. There will be male tendencies trying to harmonize with a female body and social pressures to change.

Seth explains that Carl Jung's theory of anima and animus can be understood in reincarnational terms.

«The anima in the male is, therefore, the psychic memory and identification of all the previous female existences in which the inner self has been involved. It contains within it the knowledge of the present male's past female histories, and the intuitive understanding of all the female qualities with which the personality is innately endowed. The anima, therefore, is an important safeguard, preventing the male from over-identifying with whatever cultural male characteristics have been imposed upon him through present background, environment, and civilization».

The animus then is the soul's memory of all the male existences and is the balancing mechanism for those souls occupying female bodies.

g) Habits, character and interests, as well as vocational talents can have their basis in past life development. Take the extreme example of Schlieman, the German, who from an early age was obsessed with an interest in Ancient Greece and specifically Troy. He amassed a fortune and came to Greece to uncover the cities of Troy of which he «knew» the location. Or consider T.E. «Lawrence of Arabia», an Englishman who had such a «feeling» for being an Arab.

In addition to these extreme examples, many people find, at various stages in their lives, that they have a talent for activities that they have never «studied» in this life. The Cayce readings often put people in touch with abilities which they never knew they had. With very little effort they excelled in these fields once they had opened their minds to the possibility.

h) We have all experienced **love at first sight** and, of course, repulsion at first sight. These can be very reasonably explained by encounters with these souls in the dramas of previous lives. In fact most of our close relationships are with souls who have been with us before. This was emphasized over and over again in the Cayce readings.

Seth expresses the same truth:

«Families have subconscious purposes, though the individual members of the family may pursue these goals without conscious awareness. Such groups are set up ahead of time, so to speak, in-between physical existences. Often four or five individuals will set themselves a given challenge and assign to the various members different parts to play. Then in a physical existence the roles will be worked out».

Close relationships are formed by love, fear and hate. We will find ourselves married to the very beings with whom we are deeply attached or detest. Always there are lessons. Those who are your friends or enemies now may be your mother, father, child, wife or husband in a future life. If we don't learn to get along with certain people now, then we can be sure that we will encounter them again until we learn to forgive, have compassion and harmonize the relationship."

Helen Wambach, as already mentioned, has guided 750 subjects back into past memories through hypnosis. Among many of the revealing questions she asked them was, «did you know any of your present close relations in past lives?» Fully 87% answered **yes.** Here are a few of the answers as presented in Ms. Wambach's book Life Before Life.

(Case A-203) «I knew that my mother was a fellow student at one time, and we had had a very happy companionship. My father was once my older brother who was dull. It seems we made fun of his dullness in a previous life».

(Case A-460) «My mother was a close male friend from a past life.

*My father was my wife whom I used to treat cruelly in a past life».
(Case A-389) «My mother was my mother in a lifetime in 500 BC
and I didn't necessarily like her then either».*

Dr. Raymond Moody's studies on patients who have been clinically
declared dead and then have come back to life, are supplying much
evidence for the existence of life after death as compiled in his book
Life after Life. Ms. Wambach's studies are supporting the fact of
Life Before Life. If the consciousness exists after life and before
life, then it most probably exists in-between lives.

Most religions accept that the soul will exist eternally, that it will
have no end. Anything that is without end must also be without
beginning. So, what has the soul been doing all this time? Waiting
to be born for only one life?

GUIDING OTHERS INTO MEMORIES
OF THEIR PAST LIVES

I have personally guided about 250 people into memories of their
past lives with the aid of a special procedure available to all called
«Awareness Techniques». Although I did not record the results in
the way that Ms. Wambach did, many are recorded on tape and
they correlate completely with hers.

Guiding these people through these detailed memories of their
actions, thoughts, feelings, relationships, scenery and general
characteristics of previous lives was perhaps, for me, the most
convincing personal experience leading me to believe in
reincarnation. Some of these individuals did not believe in
reincarnation at the start of the session.

One very interesting point was that 95% of my subjects enjoyed the
process of death, when they let go of the body and experienced the
freedom of being a spirit without a body. No matter how horrifying
the death circumstances (and some of them were literally writhing
with sweat and fear while remembering) when the body was
dropped, there was only peace and bliss. Some remained around to
watch the funeral, if there was one. Some tried, futilely, to contact

their loved ones who were mourning, to try to inform them that mourning was unnecessary, that they were fine. The living mourn for themselves and their own loss. The dead are fine.

On the other hand the birth process was one of great discomfort and suffering. Can you imagine fitting a free spirit in that tiny, uncoordinated, helpless body, at mercy of so many unconscious adults? We have already referred to Ms. Wambach's subjects' description of their birth experience into their present life. Here are a few more.

(Case A-314) «*In the birth canal I seemed to be straining and pressing on some kind of hard muscular surface. It seems I can't wait to be born. As soon as I emerged I felt a great feeling of separation, and no more warmth and protection. The people in the delivery room were kind but efficient, and I felt distance from them*».

(Case 396) «*In the birth canal, the contractions were pulses behind me. I feel long and slippery. After I'm born my feelings are that I'm tired and not too happy, and I'm still hesitant about this life. I'm very aware of two bright lights and cold, and feel away from everyone*».

(Case A-406) «*In the birth canal I felt tight and very constricted and I was aware of darkness. As soon as I emerged I saw very bright lights and heard loud noises. As soon as I was born I was aware of other people's feelings. I was surprised to find that my mother didn't want me. People were impersonal. I think to myself, «This is going to be a lonely trip». I think I must have rushed into this life*».

Thus we can clearly see that for most, birth is a rather unpleasant experience, a movement from a more pleasant state to an unpleasant state.

«In order to be born here, you must die somewhere else».

Obviously this possibility of memory of past lives and birth experiences offers an extremely valuable psychological tool for releasing subconscious traumas originating in those experiences which distort the present life perceptions and expression. It is being used today and will be used increasingly so in the future. Various techniques have been developed for releasing past life and birth traumas.

CASE STUDIES OF CHILDREN
WITH MEMORY OF PAST LIVES

There are thousands of cases of children who remember their past lives, usually the one just previous to the present. Although this happens in all countries and among all religions, in most cases, the children are told to be quiet and not make up stories. However, in countries and cultures where the concept is accepted by the adult population, the child is allowed to express itself.

I personally know individuals in the Druze villages of Lebanon who remember their past lives as children and still remember and know now some of their children from the previous life who are now, of course, much older than them. One such case, of Saada Hatoum has been presented to you in chapter IV.

Dr. Ian Stevenson of Virginia University in America has published two books on studies of such children (**Twenty Cases Suggestive of Reincarnation** and **Ten Cases Suggestive of Reincarnation).**

Drs. Satwant Pasricha and Vindoha Murthy in India are now compiling information from rigorous tests applied to 80 such cases of past life memory. Cases are taken only if they can be verified by living beings and official government records. The following case of Shanti Devi born in Delhi, India in 1926 is an example of such research. The following excerpt is taken from the book **Reincarnation in the Twentieth Century,** edited by Martin Ebon.

«*When she had reached the age of three her parents were amused because she consistently spoke of her husband and her children.*

«She will be an early bride», her father said. «We must begin setting aside her dowry. Only today I bought her a golden bangle for that day».

«Her childish talk makes me very happy», her mother said, «for she must see the joy in our lives and, as children do, wish to copy it».

«As the months rolled along Shanti spoke more and more of her «husband» and «children». Her obsession with the subject, her projection away from childish matters concerned her parents.

«Who», her mother asked, «is this husband you always mention?»

«My husband's name is Kedarnath», Shanti answered without hesitating. «He lives in Muttra. Our house is yellow stucco with large arched doors and lattice-work window. Our yard is large and filled with marigolds and jasmine. Great bowers of scarlet bougainvilleas climb over the house. We often sit on the verandah watching our little son play on the tile floor».

«Shanti's mother and father became increasingly concerned. They sensed they were not dealing with a normal child. With an overwhelming fear that their daughter was mad, they took to their family physician.

«Dr. Reddy, who had been alerted to the problem, assured the parents that Shanti was very likely an overly brilliant child who was using this kind of conversation to draw the attention to herself. He would, he said, by the sheer power of his position as a doctor, get the little girl to confess that she was living a fairy tale.

«Shanti, wrapped in a child's silk sari, hoisted herself into the doctor's hard wooden chair and sat with her hands folded whilst she answered his questions. She repeated the things she had told her parents before.

«Then how are you here – just a little girl?« the doctor asked.

«Oh, you see», Shanti answered, «my name is Ludgi and I died about a year ago. I died giving birth to another child».

«The doctor exchanged glances with her parents.

«Go on», he said, «tell us more about it».

«Shanti sighed. «It was a very difficult pregnancy from the first», she said. «I had not been well and when I knew the baby was coming I wondered if I was ready for it. Each day I felt worse and worse – and then when the baby came it was a breech birth. The baby lived but the delivery killed me».

«To each of the doctor's questions, she gave specific details. Shanti was taken out of the doctor's office by a nurse while the doctor conferred with the parents. It was impossible, they all agreed, for this only child, reared away from the gossip of Delhi, to have the mental and physical aspects of a difficult pregnancy so accurately in her mind.

«During the next four years, the bewildered parents took her from one doctor to another. Each one was fascinated but could come up with no feasible explanation for the consistent story she told.

«When Shanti was eight, her granduncle, Professor Kishen Chand, decided to take matters into his own hands. It was obvious that the girl could not be shaken from her account. It was high time to do some detective work, to find out if there were a man named Kedarnath in Muttra who, in 1925, had lost a wife named Ludgi from childbirth. Consequently, he wrote a letter filled with pertinent questions and mailed it to the address that Shanti had so often mentioned during questioning.

«When the letter arrived in Muttra, it was opened and read by a shaken widower named Kedarnath. The facts were startling to say the least, for indeed he still grieved for his dead wife. However, even as a devout Hindu, he could not accept the fact that Ludgi had been reborn, was now living in Delhi and possessed such an accurate testimony of their life together.

«Suspecting a plot, some dark plan perhaps intended to rob him of property, Kedarnath wrote to his cousin, Mr. Lal, in Delhi, asking him to meet Shanti and her family. The cousin had often been in Kedarnath's home when Ludgi was alive, and his questions would certainly prove the child to be an impostor or her parent sly blackmailers.

«On the pretext of business, Mr. Lal made appointment with Mr. Devi at his home. When Mr. Lal arrived, Shanti, then nine, was helping her mother prepare her evening meal of vegetable curry. She darted to open the door when she heard him rapping.

«Mrs. Devi caught the sound of a muffled scream and rushed to determine the cause. Shanti had thrown herself in the arms of the astonished visitor.

«Mother», she sobbed, «this is a cousin of my husband! He lived not far from us in Muttra and then moved to Delhi. I am so happy to see him! He must come in. I want to know about my husband and sons».

«At that moment Mr. Devi arrived, and the four entered the house for what turned out to be an unbelievable and confusing conference. Mr. Lal confirmed all the facts Shanti had given over the years. There was Kedarnath who had married a young woman, Ludgi. This wife gave birth to two sons, the younger of whom she was inordinately fond until her death bearing a third boy. Shanti kept nodding agreement as Mr. Lal talked.

«Professor Chand was called to join the group, to help plan their next move. They unanimously decided that Kedarnath and the favorite boy should come to Delhi as guests of the Devis.

«On their arrival, Kedarnath's son was almost rushed off his feet by the girl, smaller than he, who tried to pick him up, smothered him with kisses and called him by her own pet names which had almost been lost from the child's memory. Shanti treated Kedarnath in the mature manner of a dutiful wife and insisted on serving him biscuits and cheese with the same winsome ceremony so typical of Ludgi. As Kedarnath watched, his eyes filled with tears. This distressed Shanti who tried to console him, using endearing little phrases known only to Kedarnath and Ludgi.

«Despite Shanti's pleading, Kedarnath refused to leave his son with the Devi family. Instead, secretly frightened by the strange events, father and boy returned to Muttra to think things over.

«Reports of the unnatural affair reached the ears of Desh Bandu Gupta, president of the All-India Newspaper Association and a member of the Indian Parliament. He conferred with other responsible reporters and scientists and it was decided that if the Shanti case were a hoax, it should be exposed. If, on the other hand, the child were the reincarnation of Ludgi or if she possessed some occult power that gave her such detailed information, then India was witnessing one of the most exceptional phenomena in modern history.

«In any event, more investigation was in order. They deemed the most conclusive technique was to take Shanti to Muttra and to have her lead them to the house in which she claimed to have lived and died.

A small retinue boarded the train bound for Muttra: Shanti, her parents, Mr. Gupta, an advocate by the name of Tara C. Mathur, along with eminent scholars, scientists, reporters and several well-educated interested citizens.

«As the train puffed to a stop Shanti gave a squeal of delight and began waving to several people on the platform. Correctly, she explained they were the mother and brother of her husband. Once off the train she talked with them and questioned them, using not the Hindustani she had been taught in Delhi but the dialect of the Muttra district.

«The visitors from Delhi got into the waiting carriages and began what they felt was one of the greatest tests of all – whether or not Shanti could find her way to the alleged home. Following the child's instructions they wound through the streets dodging the streams of pedestrians and the white sacred cows that lay sleeping peacefully in the doorways or munching vegetables from the open stalls. Twice Shanti seemed doubtful which turn to make, asked for time to think and then gave her definite directions.

«At last she asked them to stop. «This is the house», she said, «but it is a different color. In my days it was yellow; now it is white».

«The facts were correct. Kedarnath and his boys no longer lived there, and the new occupants, wanting nothing to do with such eerie publicity, refused to let the investigating committee on their property.

«At Shanti's request, she was taken to the house where Kedarnath then resided. Once there, she called the two boys by name, but did not recognize the child whose birth had cost Ludgi's life.

«The next stop was at the home of Ludgi's mother, an ancient lady who was both confused and terrified by this young girl who acted like Ludgi, talked like Ludgi and knew things only Ludgi knew. Yet, as a grieving mother, she remembered every detail of her daughter's death and funeral. It was far too perplexing for her old, tired mind to grasp.

«When Shanti was asked if anything had changed on her mother's property, the youngster promptly announced that the well was no longer there. Mr. Gupta dug where she said it once was and found the well, covered with planks and dirt.

«Kedarnath asked Shanti what Ludgi had done with several rings she had hidden shortly before her death. Shanti responded that they were in a pot and buried in the garden of the old home in which they had lived. The investigating committee found them in the spot Shanti designated.

«In the days that followed this amazing and successful journey, there were no solutions forthcoming. The case stood at a stalemate with no scientific answers. There was, however, international publicity and much excitement in both Delhi and Muttrad which *proved embarrassing as well as annoying. Crowds assembled outside the Devi home as well as Kedarnath's. People stared at the young girl, pointed their fingers and whispered. Obviously, Shanti could not take up her role as mother to boys who were older than she, and her beloved Kedarnath approached her with apprehension, not affection.*

«*Shanti realized she was living in two worlds and that, while the past was appealing, it was also more painful and impossible than the present. She took the advice of others and slowly, arduously and agonizingly, Shanti mentally rejected her love of her family in Muttra and began to shape her life as a young woman in Delhi*».

During her «test» Shanti made 24 correct statements and no incorrect ones concerning her previous life as Ludgi.

An even more public and well-recorded example of past life memory is that of the Dalai Lama, the head of the Tibetan Buddhists. The present one is the 14th incarnation of the same soul who repeatedly returns to the same office and tasks. Before he dies a set of tests and agreements are made for verifying his new body at the early age of three years. Here is the test as described by Rayor Johnson Phd. in his article the **Wheel of Birth and Death.**

"Following the indications of the thirteenth Dalai Lama before he died, in which he designated the district where he expected to be reborn, a committee was set up to make a search. They found a three-year-old boy who appeared to fit their expectations. The committee then interviewed him and brought with them two identical black rosaries, one of which had belonged to the thirteenth Dalai Lama. When they offered these to him, the boy chose the one which had been his in the past life and put it around his neck. A similar test was then completed successfully with two yellow rosaries. They offered him two drums, a very small one used for calling attendants, and an ornate, attractive drum with golden straps. He chose the former and began to beat it in the way which is customary during prayers. Finally, they presented him with two walking sticks. The boy touched the first one and looked at it with some hesitation. Then he took the other and held it firmly

in his hands. The hesitation had apparently arisen because of an interesting circumstance, for the former Dalai Lama had originally used the walking stick but had subsequently given it to another Lama".

SPIRITUAL TEACHERS

In my search, I have come in contact with many teachers; some famous spiritual beings, others friends, relatives and acquaintances, and some complete strangers. I have been extremely fortunate to have contact with such inspirational beings as Swami Satchitananda, Swami Chidananda, Swami Vishnudevananda, Swami Satyananada, Richard Alpert (Ram Dass), Satya Sai Baba and many others through lectures and books. They have all taught me the truth of the principles of Reincarnation, Karma, and the Evolution of Consciousness.

Among the great occidental thinkers who embraced the concept of reincarnation were Pythagoras, Socrates, and Plato, Europeans like Shelley, Tennyson, Browning, Rossetti, Giordano, Geothe, Schopenhauer, as well as Longfellow, Walt Witman and Emerson and early Christian Founders such as Origen, Justin Martyr, St. Jerome, Clemens Alexandrinus, and Plotinus. These are a few of those of the West.

Whereas the West has excelled in its understanding of matter, the East has mastered the understanding of our relationship to the universe. From the East, and all of its great thinkers, rises an unanimous **yes** with respect to the truth of reincarnation.

OBSERVING THE LAWS OF NATURE

My engineering and science education taught me that there are basic laws operating in the universe. I have always been fascinated by the delicate intricacy with which the universe and the beings residing in it are related. To the mind attuned to the subtle order underlying this apparent chaos, a walk in the forest is certainly more exciting than an emotionally degrading film. For those of you who would like to tune into this fascinating reality of ours, I suggest the book **Supernature** by Lyall Watson.

The same laws are operating on all levels, physical, mental and spiritual. «As above, so below». For example Newton's laws of motion states that for every action or force, there is an equal and opposite action or force moving in the opposite direction. When we expand this law to include thoughts, words, and human actions, then we have the law of Karma. *«As you sow, so shall you reap».*

Albert Einstein, who was a deeply spiritual being, advanced our knowledge of the relationship between matter and energy. Now we know that matter is simply condensed energy and energy is expanded and excited matter. We have learned that there can never be any loss of matter or energy in the universe. This is called the Law of Conversation of Energy and Matter.

Obviously, if energy and matter cannot be diminished, neither can consciousness which is even more essential. Consciousness controls energy, which controls matter. For example, you see a piece of fruit, your consciousness directs the energy to your hand, which moves your physical hand which picks up the fruit.

Consciousness is independent of matter. It can exist within or without it. We call consciousness imprisoned in matter «Life», and consciousness freed from matter «Death». Strange, isn't it?

All of nature operates in cycles and rhythms. We have the seasons, the years, the days, the cycles of the moon, the cycles of the ages. We have the cycle of life within the tree. Minerals are absorbed from the earth and combined with CO_2, water and sunlight to form leaves and fruits. In the autumn, these leaves and fruits fall and either decompose on the ground or in the digestive system of some animal or insect. All become mineral again, the leaves, the fruit and animals and insects. The tree reabsorbs them and forms new leaves and fruit. The life force of the animals and insects use these new leaves and fruit to create new bodies. On and on it goes. Life never stops; it only changes form.

Here a few quotes on this subject from the Baha'i Faith
This composite association of the elements in the form of a human body is therefore subject to disintegration which we call death, but

after disintegration the elements themselves persist unchanged
Therefore total annihilation is an impossibility, and existence can
never become non-existence. This would be equivalent to saying
that light can become darkness, which is manifestly untrue and
impossible. As existence can never become non-existence, there is
no death for man; nay, rather, man is everlasting and everliving...
Throughout these degrees of its traversing the kingdoms from one
form of phenomenal being to another, it retains its atomic
existence and is never annihilated nor relegated to non-existence.

(Compilations, Baha'i World Faith, p. 263)

Non-existence therefore is an expression applied to change of
form, but this transformation can never be rightly considered
annihilation, for the elements of composition are ever present and
existent as we have seen in the journey of the atom through
successive kingdoms, unimpaired; hence there is no death; life is
everlasting. So to speak, when the atom entered into the
composition of the tree, it died to the mineral kingdom, and when
consumed by the animal, it died to the vegetable kingdom, and so
on until its transference or transmutation into the kingdom of
man; but throughout its traversing it was subject to
transformation and not annihilation. Death therefore is
applicable to a change or transference from one degree or
condition to another.

(Compilations, Baha'i World Faith, p. 264)

Water is the basis of life. Consider its cycle. It descends to earth as
rain, landing in all and various places. It flows into various rivulets,
eventually into streams, and finally into mighty rivers flowing
towards the sea. Each particle of water is like an individual soul. It
will take a different path to the sea. Some will go ahead on over the
waterfalls, others will prefer side streams, others will get caught in
stagnant pools. Some will evaporate into the air before reaching the
ocean. But, regardless of the path, all will reach the ocean. And
there they will ascend into the heavens, only to re-gather into
heavenly clouds and return to the earth again for another journey.
Sleeping, waking sleeping, waking, night and day, so flows the

rhythm of activity and rest which rules all the universe. And so flows life and death. Just as waking turns into sleeping, and sleeping into waking; so does life turn into death and death turn into life. Here is how the ancient Greek philosopher Socrates explained this argument to his student Cebes:

PHAEDO 71A-72B

«Very well, then», said Socrates, «I will state one pair of opposites which I mentioned just now; the opposites themselves and the processes between them and you shall state the other. My opposites are sleeping and waking, and I say that waking comes from sleeping and sleeping from waking, and that the processes between them are going to sleep and waking up. Does that satisfy you», he asked, «or not?»

«Perfectly».

«Now you tell me in the same way», he went on, «about life and death. Do you not admit that death is the opposite of life?»

«I do».

«And that they come from one another?»

«Yes»

«Then what comes from the living?»

«The dead»

«And what», asked Socrates, «comes from the dead?»

«I must admit», he said, «that it is the living»

«So it is from the dead, Cebes, that living things and people come?»

«Evidently»

«Then our souls do exist in the next world»

«So it seems»

«And one of the two processes in this case is really quite certain – dying is certain enough, isn't it?»

«Yes, it is», said Cebes.

«What shall we do then? Shall we omit the complementary process and leave a defect here in the law of nature? Or must we supply an opposite process to that of dying?»

«Surely we must supply it», he said.

«And what is it?»

«Coming to life again»

«Then if there is such a thing as coming to life again», said

Socrates, «it must be a process from death to life?»
«Quite so».
«So we agree upon this too: that the living have come from the
dead no less than the dead from the living. But think we decided
that if this was so, it was a sufficient proof that the souls for the
dead must exist in some place from which they are reborn».

Darwin's **theory of evolution** is common knowledge to most of
the world today. Most accept that there is sufficient evidence that
an evolution of material bodies took place from one-cell organisms,
through plants, fish and reptiles into animals, primates and then
man. What is to make us think this process has come to an end? Are
we perfect? Christ said that we cannot enter the kingdom of heaven
until we are perfect.

Scientists tell us that we use 10% of our brain. We have many lives
to go before coming perfect enough to enter the kingdom of heaven.
We have come here to express the full soul potential of the Christ
Consciousness while in the human form, and that will take many
more lifetimes of practice and learning. Evolution continues
physiologically, psychologically, and spiritually. We continue to
learn to grow. There is no end.

When we stop learning, that is real «death». Death not our leaving
the body – but rather – stopping to grow. Better to give up the body
and take a new one than to stop growing, and evolving.
Remember the poem by **Rumi:**

«I died as mineral and became plant,
I died as plant and rose to animal,
I died as animal and I was man,
Why should I fear?
When was I less by dying?»
Yet once more I shall die as man, to soar
With angels blest; but even from angelhood
I must pass on: all except God doth perish.
When I have sacrificed my angel soul,
I shall become what no mind e 'er conceived.
Oh, let me not exist! For Non-existence

Proclaims in organ tones:
«To Him we shall return».

QUESTIONS AND ARGUMENTS
AGAINST REINCARNATION

Some westerners have a built-in conditioning against a belief in this supposedly oriental concept. Many can be the arguments against it, and, as with any philosophical subject, we can all call forth those facts which support our perceptions. Here one point of view is being presented. It may or may not be true. Only you can decide that by leaving your mind open and free from your previous conditioning. Observe life as you see it today. Take a fresh look at life, and see what you see. Do not agree or disagree, but leave it on a shelf in your mind and wait for more information before making a judgment.

One common protest is, **«why don't we remember our past lives»**. There are few answers to the question. One is that many people **do** remember, and more and more are doing so each day; especially children, psychically oriented individuals and those who are undergoing hypnosis for that purpose.

Remembrance of past lives is a natural outgrowth of an evolution of consciousness, and many spiritually advanced persons know about their previous existences.

Another point is that we really do not remember very much of this life. Just because you cannot remember what you did on February 6 1953 doesn't mean that you did not exist on that day. Because you cannot remember being 2 years old does not mean that you were never two years old.

This is actually a blessing. Our mind has enough problems to deal with in our present life, without being haunted by all the experiences of relationships, conflicts and deaths of previous lives. When we can truly see ourselves as souls and not as bodies, then we will be ready and able to see our past lives in a detached way as we might watch a drama. For the unenlightened person to become aware that he killed his present wife or mother in another drama in a past life, would be a shattering experience.

Another argument put forth against reincarnation, is that of **"heredity"**. One might say that the traits of an individual are dedicated by the parents' genes and not by the being's past actions.

But we would ask, what caused that soul to be born to that particular person? Who caused that particular combination of genes (one sperm of trillions, one ovum of thousands) to combine? Also why do **identical twins** develop distinct personalities even at birth when all hereditary and environmental factors are the same? Identical twins who underwent hypnotic regression in Ms. Wambach's research found that they had had different lives, but had been very close and chose to be born together in their present life for some purpose.

Edgar Cayce explains, *«You have inherited most from yourself, not from your family. The family is only a river through which the soul flows».*

Seth reaffirms this truth:

«Each inner self, adopting a new body, imposes upon it and upon its entire genetic makeup, memory of past physical forms in which it has been involved. Now the present characteristics usually overshadow the past ones. They are dormant, but the other characteristics are latent and present, built into the pattern. The physical pattern of the present body, therefore, is genetic memory of the self's past physical forms and of their strengths and weaknesses».

For example I know a woman who always has problems with her neck and throat – that is her weak point when she is tired or ill. In a psychic reading she found that she had been beheaded in a previous life.

Many Christians experience a conflict between the official church stance and the concept of reincarnation. But for one, who wants to look, there are many sayings of Jesus that can be interpreted as a positive argument for reincarnation.

Before looking at them, may it be pointed out that as with all great spiritual teachers, there was one set of teachings for those close disciples who were more spiritually evolved, and another for the masses. Perhaps Jesus felt that the masses were not yet ready for this concept, or perhaps it was the early church fathers who removed those passages from their own reasons. Edgar Cayce's «Source» indicated the latter.

Edgar Cayce explains that in 531 AD at a Council of Church Leaders they deleted those sentences having to do with this concept:

«The readings say that when the Leaders of the early church decided to propagate the faith to all people, indiscriminantly, they decided to drop the doctrine of reincarnation. It was difficult to explain, for one thing, and it was difficult to swallow for another. It made life more complex. It made virtue even more necessary. A man had to be pretty brave to face the fact that one life of suffering was only a step toward heaven».

Even if they did remove most of the passages concerning reincarnation, they overlooked some that certainly hint at it. One is recorded in Matthew chapters 11 and 17 where the disciples ask why Elias had not come yet as prophesized.

And Jesus answered:
«But I say to you, that Elias has come already, and they knew him not, and they did to him whatsoever they wanted».

«Then the disciples understood that he spoke to them of John the Baptist».

How could John the Baptist be Elias unless he was a reincarnation of Elias?

In the 3rd chapter of John, Jesus said to Nicodemus,
*«Unless a man be **born again** he cannot see the kingdom of*

heaven».

And in the 5th chapter of Matthew, He says,
«Unless a man **be perfect** *he cannot enter the kingdom of heaven»*.

Who can become perfect in one lifetime? Perhaps he was telling us that we had to be born again and again in order to become perfect enough to enter the kingdom of heaven.

When the disciples asked Jesus about the man who was born blind, they asked, *«who did sin, this man, or his parents, that he was born blind»* (John 9th chapter).

They obviously believed in Karma for they were sure that his blindness was due to a sin. So they held to the concept that suffering is a result of some past cause. And they must have believed in reincarnation, for how could a newborn blind baby have sinned unless in a past existence?

Edgar Cayce read the <u>Bible</u> cover to cover every year and was very familiar with its details. He points another interesting passage.

«This is from Revelation, 13th chapter, 10th verse. He that leads into captivity shall go into captivity: he that killeth with the sword will be killed with the sword. Here is the patience and faith of saints.

«Certainly every man who killed another with a sword wasn't killed by a sword himself – not in the same life. And what is the patience and faith of the saints but an understanding that surpasses man's understanding, and leaves justice to God's law?»

This brings to mind the blind university professor who went to Edgar Cayce for a life reading and found that his present condition was the result of a lifetime in Persia where he burned the eyes of the enemies with a hot iron.

After Job had lost all his possessions and children and came down with a horrible disease of the skin, he undauntedly spoke to the Lord. *«Teach me, and I will hold my tongue, and cause me to understand wherein I have erred»*. He had the «patience and faith of the saints», and knew that he was suffering the result of some self-committed error, or Karma.

Regardless of whether we accept reincarnation or not, the message is the same whether from Jesus the Christ, the Buddha or the Hindu Scriptures.

«As you sow, so shall you reap». *«Do unto others as you would have them do to you»*. Jesus the Christ.

«Hurt not others in ways that you yourself would find hurtful». The Buddha.

«This is the sum of duty; to naught unto others which cause pain if done to you». Hindu Scriptures.

«There is only One Religion. The religion of LOVE». Sri Satya Say Baba

POSSIBLE THERAPIES AND
ATTITUDES TOWARDS LIFE

I began this chapter with a statement of how confused, lonely and depressed I felt before embracing the concept of reincarnation, karma and evolution of consciousness. All that has disappeared. I now see that the purpose of my life is to grow and evolve in my ability to create, love and understand. Also I see that an additional purpose is to be a catalyst for others to undergo the same process.

But I had to die to my old self, which was clinging to a conditioning which was imposed on me from youth. I had to realize that I could be what I wanted to be, and would not be a complete failure if I didn't meet up to society's expectations of what was successful; i.e. money, many possessions and prestige. In other words, I went through a psychological death to my old self.

This did not happen all at once, although there were periods of more radical change than others. But mostly it was a slow bit by bit dying everyday of ego traits, attachments, habits, and concepts. This continues daily. Everyday our cells are dying and new ones are being reborn. We have a completely new body every seven years. In actuality no cell in your body is more than seven years old. We might say that your body is seven years old. But your mind makes it a lot older. The key to evolution is to constantly die to our old self. An Austrian Augustinian monk expressed it well:

«The man who dies before he dies, does not die when he dies».

Stanislov Grof, MD in his article «Transitions: Birth, Death and Rebirth" express what happens to those who go through a psychological death:

«A well-integrated death/rebirth experience gives to life of the individual the feeling that he can effortlessly participate in the creative process. A life lived with this feeling has been compared to the existence of a flower, which effortlessly utilizes the sunshine, the minerals from the soil, and the water it draws from the ground. It feels no concern over whether it is going to end in a wedding bouquet, or a salad, whether it will be eaten or stepped on by a cow, while it is alive, it just expresses the self-actualization of its own particular aspect of creation».

Techniques for providing an environment for a psychological ego-death were the basis and purpose of the ancient mystery schools such as the cult of Isis and Osiris, and the Eleusinian and Orphic cults. The Tibetans and Egyptians had their **Book of the Dead,** to guide one through death and rebirth of the ego or the body. The Catholics had the **Ars Moriendi** or the **Art of Dying.**

When we have accepted our immortal nature that we are souls, we can look at the drama of life in a more detached way, with less pain and despair. We will feel both involved and detached at the same time. We will be involved in our actions and in fulfilling our life. On the other hand, we will be detached from the results of our efforts, doing our best and leaving the results to God; knowing that each result is limited by past Karma.

The model of a bank account is a good one. We each have a «Karmic Bank Account». Selfless thoughts, words and deeds represent deposits and selfish ones are the withdrawals. If we have been making mostly withdrawals in past lives, then, although we are making many deposits in this life, it may take time for the account to balance and for us to receive any interest. So we keep on depositing those selfless acts trusting the honesty of the Cosmic Banker who will give us our interest when our account is positive.

This does not mean that one must leave all and everything up to destiny. We must act according to what we feel is right, with compassion and love for the others, working to relieve suffering whenever we can, all the time keeping in mind that those who are suffering are not «victims» but actually receiving the just return of their past acts. We love and help them to overcome their problems and we all grow and evolve in the process.

As Edgar Cayce has aptly expressed, *«That indifference to human suffering causes destiny to place it upon your own doorstep»*. This is what is called the **Sin of Omission,** in which an individual is concerned with only his own selfish needs and comforts and ignores the suffering of those around him. Such a person will find himself or herself in the same situation either in the same life or a future one, in order to be sensitized and learn sympathy, compassion and the truth of the oneness of humanity.

In this way, Karma is not so much a punishment as an opportunity to learn and evolve. The degree to which one's life is shaped by Karma will depend on the individual's past lives and how much he has learned. The state of his Karmic Bank Account will be an important factor. If we owe a lot of Karma, then we will be more limited in our degrees of freedom. If we have a surplus of good karma, then we have more freedom of choice.

It is very similar to a school. When we are in the first grade, we must do whatever the teacher says. We have no choices at all. As we graduate on the higher grades, and gain more responsibility, then we are given more choices. When we go on to the university, we can pretty much decide when we want to study, **but we still must pass the tests.**

At this stage, we must truly take responsibility not only for our choices, but also for the results of our choices. For it is through the wrong choices that we learn. We must accept that everything we are experiencing, internally and externally, is a result of our previous choices, thoughts, words, and deeds.

At this point in our evolution we must stop blaming our family, relatives, friends, society, and government for our problems. We must accept that we are in exactly the situation we deserve to be. That each experience is the next lesson in our life.

Each person with whom we have conflict must be seen as teacher who is showing us where we are holding on. Each unpleasant and pleasant experience is a lesson – an opportunity to learn. We have the **free will** to learn or not learn from our experiences.

Thomas Sugrue, author of the **Story of Edgar Cayce,** expresses in this way:

«Every person's life is shaped to some extent by Karma: his own, that of his associates and loved ones, that of his nation and race, and that of the world itself. But these, singly or together, are not greater than free will. It is what the person does about these influences and urges, how he reacts to them, that makes a difference in his soul development. Because of Karma some things are more probable than others, but so long as there is free will, anything is possible».

It will surprise many of the readers that they have chosen the parameters of their life. They have chosen to be born at this time, into those specific families, cultural and economic conditions. These are not by chance. When Ms. Wambach asked her regressed subjects whether they had chosen to be born in the late twentieth century, she received answers like these:

(Case B-12) «I felt my reason for this particular life in this time period was to have contact with particular people who also chose this time period».

(Case B-55) «I came this time to get to know my mother better who was my best friend in a previous life and she was alive in this time period».

(Case A-384) «I chose the last half of the twentieth century to be alive because more advanced spirits are being born and we are close to obtaining world peace and a sense of the total self of mankind».

(Case B-88) «I chose the late half of the twentieth century because of the transition of history from a religious to a scientific view, and at the end of this stage, a spiritual awakening».

In addition to the peace of mind and clarity of the purpose of life to be had through an acceptance of reincarnation and a knowledge of one's past lives, there are other more mundane benefits. Some of them are as follows:

a) In a regression we might experience ourselves as a man, a woman, a child, a Caucasian, a black, an Indian, a Greek, a Turk, a Chinese, a murderer, a victim, an employer and employee, a wealthy person or a beggar. In this way one can gain other perspectives on life. There would then be much less bigotry, hatred and war in the world.

b) We could experience the death process and more deeply feel the immortality of consciousness. Fear of death and mourning for lost ones would cease, and life would be more joyful.

c) As already mentioned, those whose lives are being dominated by fears, and hang-ups, having their origin in past lives, can be released from them through re-experiencing them.

d) Souls who have developed artistic, musical, intellectual, mechanical, or any such abilities in the past can get in touch with their multidimensional nature and bring forth these talents, for more personal and social fulfillment.

e) We can get a more accurate picture of what life was like during the history of our civilization and even previous civilizations like

Atlantis. The cycles of growth and decay will become more obvious and our perspective will be broader.

f) Along with the ability to enter the area of the soul memory containing these past experiences, will also come the ability to tune into future «probabilities». Although the future is open to the exercise of free will, it is also limited to some degree by past karma. We will be able to see more clearly where we are heading with certain choices.

In conclusion, my life has thus far lead me to accept the concept of reincarnation as the best possible answer so far as to the nature of my existence in this body on this earth. Perhaps my view will change in the future. Through accepting this belief my life has grown more peaceful, meaningful and creative.

«Knowing your reincarnational background, but not knowing the true nature of your present life, is useless. You cannot justify or rationalize present circumstances by saying, «This is because of something I did in past life», for within yourself now is the ability to change negative influences. You may have brought negative influences into your life for a given reason, but the reason always has to do with understanding, and understanding removes those influences».

SETH

CHAPTER VII

AN ANALYSIS OF
THE BASIS OF REALITY

«By convention there is color,
by convention sweetness,
by convention bitterness,
but in reality there are atoms and space».

Dimocritos (c. 460 - c. 400 B.C.)

The reality we perceive is subjectively influenced by our belief systems and subconscious programming. Thus each person experiences reality differently. We perceive the same events and the same people in different ways.

Take a man named John for example. To each person he is something else. To his wife, he is a husband, a lover, and a partner in life. To his children he is a father, an authority, a disciplinarian, and a representative of manhood. To his siblings he is a brother with positive and negative traits. To his parents he is a child, who gave them many lessons, and he will always be their child. To his friends he is a man who can be trusted in times of need and a person to share ideas and activities with. To his co-workers he is the man with whom they must work with eight hours a day; a man who they may know very little about. To his neighbor, he is the man of a family who makes much noise. To his enemy he is an inconsiderate slob who is the cause of all his enemy's unhappiness. To his employee, he is the insensitive boss who doesn't take his needs into consideration. To the woman looking for a mate, he is a fair game even if he is married. To himself he is a combination of all these realities which the others see, plus thousands of other internal fantasies which others do not perceive.

Thus the man John is a different reality to each person, depending on the various subjective factors involved in their relationships. What then is the *reality* of John? Who is the *permanent* John? We each perceive our own personal reality through a vast matrix of preconceptions, expectations, desires, hopes, needs, fears and subconscious conditioning that gives each person, object and event a unique form for us.

We see people in terms of their profession or political affiliation. We label them. He is a doctor, a policeman, an actor, an artist, a businessman, a communist, a capitalist, a Democrat, a Republican. Some others categorize people in terms of their astrological sign and then are satisfied that they «know them inside out». They say, he is a Cancer, a Scorpio, a Gemini, a Pisces and identify that person with some stereotyped idea of that sign which they have read in some book or magazine.

Still others experience the people around them in terms of their religious or philosophical beliefs. «He is a Christian, a Hindu, a Moslem, a Buddhist or a Jew» and they feel they know him then. Still others classify persons in terms of their physical appearance and manner of dress. The one with the blond curly hair, who wears the blue dress, with the antique silver necklace. And they now know «who she is».

Is it possible to describe who someone is in any of the above terms? Obviously not. These ways of seeing reality are partial, superficial and extremely limiting to our capacity to love and see reality as it is.

Who is this real self that we really are? Let us begin to analyze the basis of the reality which we see around us. We observe reality through our five senses. These senses bring a myriad assortment of colors, forms, sounds, tastes, smells and tactile sensations. These inputs pass through our programming and belief system and form the subjective reality which we experience. Let us take our friend John who is something different to every one. Let us analyze him in terms of what we know about physics.

1) First let us remove his clothing. We know that he can put on and take off his clothing at will and thus, cannot be his clothing. So we cannot describe his real nature in terms of his clothing or anything else he may wear on his body.

2) Now let us look at his physical body. It is made up of may trillions of tiny cells. These cells carry out the various functions which keep John's body alive. Millions of these cells are born and die each day. Thus John's reality cannot be his cells.

3) Each of these cells is made up of large molecules called DNA. These large complex DNA molecules seem to be the basic structure from which living beings are made of. These DNA molecules are made up of atoms of Carbon, Hydrogen, Oxygen and other elements. These atoms are connected together by intermolecular forces. So far we can say that John is a complex conglomeration of various atoms which are held together by the attractive forces between them.

4) What are these atoms made of? They are made of three basic particles, with many minor particles. In the center of the atom we have the nucleus, which is the basic «material» part of the atom. Extremely tiny electrons orbit around the nucleus. These electrons have virtually no mass and sometimes we cannot determine if they are waves or particles.

In order to understand how tiny an atom is, we can use the following analogy. If we took an orange and expanded it until it was the size of the Earth itself, then the atoms in the orange would be about the size of a cherry.

At the same time, the atom is mostly space. If we take the atom itself and magnify it until it becomes the size of the largest dome in the world (St. Peter's in Rome) then the nucleus in the center will be a barely visible grain of salt in the center of the huge magnified atom.

Thus the actual matter of an atom is an incredibly small speck in the center of a proportionally large space occupied by the energy field of the electrons surrounding the nucleus. *The atom is mostly space.*

Thus the physical matter we see around us is not the solid reality which our limited senses describe. It is almost entirely space, with a very little particle substance, located in the center of various force fields created by the electrons orbiting around the nucleus.

Our picture of our friend John is changing. The only thing we can say about him so far is that he is made up of a lot of space which is made up of particles and force fields.

5) But this also describes **every other object** in this universe. So at this point we can no longer differentiate John from any other body in the universe. John at this level of reality is the same as every other person, wall, tree, building, machine, insect, ocean, cloud, or mountain.

John is just protons, neutrons and electrons, like every other material object in the universe. There is no difference. We are left with a view which Democritos realized 2,400 years ago; «By convention there is color, by convention sweetness, but in reality there are atoms and space».

6) As we investigate the nucleus of the atom more deeply, we find that there are many subatomic particles moving around in there. And we come to the extremely strange realization that, in some mysterious way, these subatomic particles are coming into existence and then fading out again. They are not stable. They come into being and then disappear. At one moment they seem to be particles and in the next they appear in the form of energy. Energy seems to become matter and change back into energy. Nuclear Physicist Fritjof Capra, the author of **The Tao of Physics**, can explain this much better than I.

«Once it (matter) is seen to be a form of energy, mass is no longer required to be indestructible, but can be transformed into other forms of energy. This can happen when subatomic particles collide with one another. In such collisions, particles can be destroyed and the energy contained in their masses can be transformed into kinetic energy distributed among other particles participating in the collision. Conversely, when particles collide with very high velocities, their kinetic energy can be used to form new particles».

«These dynamic patterns, or "energy bundles", form the stable nuclear, atomic and molecular structures which build up matter and give its macroscopic solid aspect, thus making us believe that it is made of some material substance. At the macroscopic level it no longer makes sense. Atoms consist of particles and these particles are not made of any material stuff. When we observe them, we never see any substance; what we observe are dynamic patterns changing into one another – a continuous dance of energy».

7) Now we are really confused. What seemed to be our friend John has become a mass of energy, now appearing as energy and then appearing as matter. **Thus every object in the universe is nothing more than condensed energy.** This energy can express itself as energy such as heat, electricity or light, or as the bond between two particles, or as the particles themselves. Thus energy is holding more dense forms of energy together and we call it John, or a table or a wall.

8) As we continue our research into the basis of reality, we begin to discover that **particles are actually coming into existence out of the void,** out of empty space **and then disappearing again**. We have just accepted that we cannot distinguish between matter and energy and now they tell us that we may not even be able to distinguish between matter and empty space. Are these physicists or metaphysicists? I'll let Mr. Capra explain it to you:

«The distinction between matter and empty space finally had to be abandoned when it became evident that virtual particles can come into being spontaneously out of the void, and vanish again into the void, without any nucleon or other strongly interacting particle being present. According to field theory, events of that kind can happen all the time. The vacuum is far from empty. It contains an unlimited number of particles which can come into being and vanish without end».

«Here then is the closest parallel to the void of Eastern mysticism in modern physics. Like the Eastern void, the physical vacuum as it is called in field theory, is not a state of mere nothingness, but contains the potentiality for all forms of the particle world. These

forms, in turn, are not independent physical entities, but merely transient manifestations of the underlying world. As the sutra says, (Form is emptiness and emptiness is indeed form)».

*«The relationship between the virtual particles and the vacuum is essentially dynamic relation, **the vacuum is truly a «living void»**, pulsating in endless rhythms of creation and destruction. The discovery of the dynamic quality of a vacuum is seen by many physicists as one of the most important findings of modern physics. From its role of an empty container of the physical phenomena, the void has emerged as a dynamic quantity of utmost importance. The results of modern physics thus seem to confirm the words of the Chinese sage Chang Tsai:*

«When one knows that the Great Void is full of CHI, one realizes that there is no such thing as nothingness».

9) The «CHI» which the Chinese sage Chang Tsai refers to, is the *Bioenergy* (Prana to the yogis) that fills the universe. Now we get a picture in which there is this empty space which contains within it an invisible, undetectable subtle bioenergy that can at some point manifest to our senses as various forms of energy or particles or some combination of the two, i.e. a particle in motion, or a being capable of movement. Our dear friend John now appears to us as empty space, which has formed itself into various types of energies, which can be expressed as matter or energy.

We cannot distinguish John from any other object or energy in the universe. On a molecular level John is not distinguishable from any other person or object in the universe. This is the level of *Prakriti* as understood by the Yogi. **This is the basis of the material reality**.

10) But what causes this empty space to differentiate and appear as separate beings and objects such as John, Mary and the table, the wall, the car or the ocean? There are all one energy – matter conglomerate, and yet they appear different. Now we are really confused.

11) Since the first visible sign of the empty space manifesting itself is that bioenergy, let us start our investigation here. Experiments with photographic film have revealed that the bioenergy around animate and inanimate objects can be photographed.

It seems that the pictures of great holy men and saints with halos around their heads are not products of imagination. It is now scientifically proven that all beings have an aura, an energy field which surrounds and permeates their bodies.

The great name in the art of photographing the *Aura* is the Russian Kirlian from whom we get the name Kirlian photography. As this science continues to generate reproducible results, we begin to understand that this energy field is in some way linked with the being's vitality, health, and emotional and mental condition. This energy seems to be a connecting link between the systems of the body and the mind. This energy flows through specific channels in the body and even between the body and the environment. Lyall Watson comments on this in his book **Supernature**.

«*One of those to make the pilgrimage to see the Kirlians in Krasnodar was Mikhail Gaikin, a surgeon from Leningrad. After looking at the cavalcade of lights in his own hands, he began to wonder about their origin. The strongest flares shone right out of the skin like searchlights, but their positions corresponded with no major nerve endings in the body, and the pattern of their distribution showed no correspondence with arteries or veins. Then he remembered his experiences on the Zabaikal front in 1945 and the lessons he had learned from a Chinese doctor in the art of acupuncture. Acting on his hunch, he sent the Kirlians a standard acupuncture chart of seven hundred important points on the skin – and they tallied exactly with charts that the Kirlians had begun to prepare of the fires visible under their high-frequency machine*».

12) Mr. Watson, also points out other evidence which indicates that this energy field is independent of the physical body and, in some way, has the power to organize the formation and function of the cells of the body. Here he refers to his bioenergy field as «biological plasma».

«If a biological plasma body exists, I would expect it to be produced by the organism. Once it exists, it is possible that it could exercise some sort of organizational function over the body that made it. There is one study that showed that a muscle that was surgically removed from a mouse and cut up into small pieces would regenerate completely if this mince was packed back into the wound. But perhaps the best example is provided by the sponge. There are some colonies of unicellular animals that get together in large social groups, but sponges are more complex than this and are classified as single organisms. The cells in their bodies are loosely organized but occur in several forms, which fulfill different functions. There are collar cells, which live in cavities and wave whips to create the currents of water that flow through the animal's pores to bring it food and oxygen; there are sex cells, which produce eggs and sperm; and there are cells that build supporting skeletons of such superb geodesic construction that they serve as inspiration for aircraft designers. Some sponges grow to several feet in diameter, and yet, if you cut them up and squeeze the pieces through silk cloth to separate each cell from its neighbor, this gruel soon gets together and organizes itself – and the complete sponge reappears like a phoenix to go back into business again. A persistent plasma body would provide a perfect template for regeneration of this kind. Whatever it may be called, «bioplasma» or «aura» or «life field», it is becoming difficult to avoid the conclusion that our sphere of influence does not end with the skin. Beyond the traditional confines of our bodies are forces we seem to produce and may be able to control.»

13) From this new information we can begin to understand that this bioenergy (prana) which seems to appear out of the empty space has the power to give form to a being or an object. We might suppose that crystals have such fields which govern the specific way in which the crystals will be formed.

Each being has a different type of energy field or *energy body* (if you like the term) that seems to determine the qualities of the physical form or body. Other scientific experiments lead us to believe this. Kirlian photographs were taken of chicken's eggs throughout the process of development of the embryo. These photographs clearly showed that the energy field of the embryo appeared long before the actual development of the physical embryo. **The energy body seems to precede the physical body.**

14) Now as we consider our friend John, we see that he is a conglomerate of particles and energies which are given a unique form by an energy body which seems to come out of the void. **It is the energy body which forms his body into something unique and separate from the universe.**

When John «dies» that energy body leaves the physical body and that hump of material particles and energies decomposes into the earth and becomes one with the material universe again.

15) Now we want to know *where this energy has come from* and *why it has taken the specific shape* as opposed to some other type of shape. The most likely explanation for this is the mind.

The mind can cause the energy to lift the hand or cause the body to walk. When the mind is upset, the energy flows in a violent way. When the mind is relaxed, this energy has a different color and is flowing harmoniously. **As a person changes his ways of thinking, his energy body begins to go through drastic changes.** We sometimes cannot even recognize an old friend who has gone through significant philosophical changes in his life.

There are cases of healing in which one person is able to change the flow of bioenergy in the other person by thought power. This has been done in experiments with Kirlian photography.

Up to now our investigation has physics backing it up, but as we get into the mind we have to move into metaphysics for our answers. *There is much evidence that causes us to believe that the mind is involved in an intimate relationship with our energy field **that then determines our physical form.***

This may explain how some great beings, who have become masters of their own bodies, energy and mind, **are able to create an object by simply thinking of it**. The thought form causes the energy to

184 The Mystical Circle of Life

gather out of the void, and physical matter condenses around the energy field in order to form the object. It seems logical enough in terms of what we have discussed so far. *We can imagine that the thought is like steam, which condense into water (energy), which freezes into ice (matter).*

16) Now we are going to have to proceed with speculation and help from those who have tread before us. There are beings who have investigated the mind and what is beyond it and at the base of it from within. They are the many yogis, mystics, saints and great thinkers whose findings are quite consistent with one another and probably are more in agreement than the various schools of nuclear physics today.

Great scientists today, after penetrating through the illusion of matter, have been very understandably accepting the age-old answers upon which all religions and spiritual philosophies are based. Here an article called «SCIENTISTS IN SEARCH OF THE SOUL» by John Gliedman printed in Science Digest (July 1982) refers to the ideas embraced by Sir. John Eccles, the great physiologist and winner of the 1963 Nobel Prize for Physiology for his research on the nerve synapse.

«Eccles strongly defends the ancient religious belief that human beings consist of a mysterious compound of physical matter and intangible spirit. Each of us embodies a nonmaterial thinking and perceiving self that «entered» our physical brain sometimes during embryological development or very early childhood, says the man who helped lay the cornerstones of modern neurophysiology.

«This «ghost in the machine» is responsible for everything that makes us distinctively human: conscious self-awareness, free will, personal identity, creativity and even emotions such as love, fear and hate. Our nonmaterial self controls its «liaison brain» the way a driver steers a car or a programmer directs a computer. Man's ghostly spiritual presence, says Eccles, exerts just the whisper of a physical influence on the computer-like brain, enough to encourage some neurons to fire and others to remain silent.

«Boldly advancing what for most scientists is the greatest heresy of all, Eccles also asserts that our nonmaterial self survives the death of the physical brain. Eccles is not the only world-famous scientist taking a controversial new look at the ancient mind-body conundrum. From Berkeley to Paris and from London to Princeton, prominent scientists from fields as diverse as neurophysiology and quantum physics are coming out of the closet and admitting that they believe in the possibility at least of such unscientific entities as the immortal human spirit and divine creation».

17) Now what do we see when we look at John? We can imagine that there is an *immortal human spirit* that is imperceptible to our physical senses. According to Yoga Philosophy and most religious teachings, this Spirit has no physical qualities such as sex, age, nationality, race, etc. It is *pure consciousness, eternal existence* and *unending bliss.* We cannot prove this to our physical senses. We are, however, told by those who have made it their life pursuit, to investigate the mind and transcend it from within, that **we are indeed immortal spirits that have manifested these minds and bodies.**

So it seems that *Spirit* permeates the empty space and at a particular time and place (in relationship to our senses) *projects a mind*, which forms an *energy body* in the womb of a chosen female. **This energy body governs the combination of genes which produce the unique self which we call John.** This spirit supports the existence of this mind and energy body through their growth and development in the physical world until the physical vehicle is no longer useful.

18) From the point of view of Yoga Philosophy the **Universal Spirit occupies all space. It is like space itself, undisturbed by the events taking place within it**. Space is not in anyway changed by the formation of an object in it or the movement of an object through it. **In the same way the spirit is unaffected by the objects and movements occurring within its being.**

For some reason, which is not easily comprehended, the universal, omnipresent, immortal spirit enters into relationship with matter (Prakriti). Each religion has its own mythology representing this process of the One becoming many, and the descent of spirit into matter. All religions agree that this has happened, but each uses another story to explain the reason and process. These stories are communicated in terms of a space-time relationship, which exists in our minds, and not in the ultimate reality. Metaphysics points out that time and space are creations of the human mind. Modern science also agrees. Let us refer again to Fritjof Capra's book **Tao of Physics**:

«The real revolution that came with Einstein's theory... was this: the abandonment of the idea that space-time coordinate system has objective significance as a separate physical entity. Instead of this, relativity theory implies that the space and time coordinates are only the elements of language that is used by an observer to describe his environment».

«This is indeed an entirely new situation. Every change of coordinate systems mixes space and time in a mathematically well-defined way. The two can therefore no longer be separated because what is space to one observer will be a mixture of time and space to another observer. Relativity theory has shown that space is not three-dimensional and time is not a separate entity. Both are intimately and inseparably connected and form a four-dimensional continuum which is called «space-time».

This concept of space-time was introduced by Hermann Minkowski in a famous lecture in 1908 with the following words:

«The views of space and time which I wish to lay today before you having sprung from the solid of experimental physics, and therein lies their strength. They are radical. Henceforth space by itself and time by itself, are doomed to fade away into mere shadows, and only a kind of union of the two will preserve an independent reality».

19) We are trying to explain an event such as the beginning of the process of creation which has no beginning and is not limited by time and space in any way. Creation and destruction, expansion and absorption are taking place continuously and endlessly. The concept of *beginning* and *end* is something created by our limited minds which makes the reason and process of the «One becoming the many» and the interacting of spirit and matter incomprehensible to us. We may understand it only through direct mystical experience, in which the rational mind is transcended. Thus we are forced to accept the answers given by those who have had such mystical experiences.

20) Their answers are something like the following:

The Universal Spirit manifests itself as the many individual spirits. We may imagine this to be like the one cell which divides into two. The second is exactly like the same. The first has not been diminished in any way by its becoming two. The two become four and so forth until we have the billions of individual cells or spirits.

The concept of the flame may also help us. One flame exists. A second candle is lit from the first, and then billions of candles are lit from the first self-lighting flame. The first flame exists now as all of the billions of candles lit from that same flame lightning up many bodies. The same Divine Spirit is vitalizing life force of all the trillions of beings.

21) When an individual spirit wants to incarnate onto the earth and enter into relationship with matter, it must form around itself a series of bodies or instruments with which to interact with the physical world. The type of body the spirit will project will depend on the memories or impressions recorded in the spirit's previous interaction with the material world. These will determine whether the spirit will project the body of a plant, animal, human or other type of living being.

The characteristics of the individual will also be determined by those characteristics developed in the spirit's previous experience here on the earth. This is the source of uniqueness. This is what makes John appear different from all the other beings on the earth – his accumulation of tendencies or impressions from past lives.

Remember the first cell which separated into two. These two cells then started to have different experiences. These experiences caused them to develop throughout the ages, different qualities in harmony with Darwin's concept of evolution and the survival of the fittest. In the same way, each spirit has experienced a unique set of past experiences in our evolutionary pattern. This causes our expression of our character in the human body to appear unique from all other beings. Thus *the cause of the illusion of our separateness lies in our **different experiences*** and the reactions to those experiences that are stored in our soul-memory (in the causal body).

22) Thus, John is one with, and indifferentiable from, all the universe on the atomic level, the energy level and the spiritual level. The illusion of difference starts in the mind, which is affected by the impressions of the causal body.

This mental programming causes a unique formation in the energy body which causes the unique body which we call John. The mind's identification with the impressions stored in its deep subconscious and with the physical body (which is the result of those impressions) is the cause of the feeling of difference and separateness which we feel when we look at the world around us.

23) Let us take the example of a movie projector. There is the projection light which shines steadily. It is **pure white light**. This is the *spirit*. It is the same as all other projection lights. It has no color. It is not differentiable from any other projection light. The projection light is the individual spirit. *Pure white light itself coming from no particular source is the Universal Spirit.*

This light then passes through the film. The **film** is the *mind*. The **images on the film** are the *samskaras* or *impressions in the soul memory*. The **changing pattern of light**, flowing toward the white projection screen, is the *energy body, or bioplasma,* or *prana,* however you would like to call it.

The **image upon the screen** is the *physical body and the world of physical events*. The unchanging white screen is the atomic reality of "Prakriti" or "Maya" according to yoga philosophy.

Thus we can understand that the projector light (the spirit) and the White Screen (the atomic reality) are the *only* permanent realities. They are the **basis of reality.** *All the changing lights, films and images are a passing show* which catch our attention and makes us believe that they are real, just as we get caught up in watching a film and *loose the awareness* of the light and of the white screen which is the basic reality.

24) The reality of the mind, energy body and physical body in their unique separate experience is only a *temporary relative reality* that is continuously changing and will end. *When it ends there will be only undifferentiated spirit and undifferentiated atomic reality.*

So the individual we call John is only a temporary phenomenon, like a wave upon the sea, which will soon fade away into the Basic Reality from which it has apparently separated itself, just as the wave fades back into the sea and loses its individual reality.

25) According to Yoga Philosophy, the atomic reality itself has emerged out of the *unmanifest God*, in the same way that Mr. Capra described the virtual particles appearing out of the void. It is believed that this atomic reality (Prakriti) exists solely for the use of the spirit (Purusha) in its evolution through matter. Theoretically all this atomic reality will be once *again reabsorbed into the unmanifest void*; as it is perhaps happening in what we call Black Holes, where great stars are collapsing into themselves and disappearing into a tremendous gravitational field.

This process of manifestation and reabsorption of the physical world supposedly **occurs rhythmically as does the coming of day and night**, or the incoming and outgoing breath. It is for this reason that we cannot talk about how it all began. Exactly, because there was no beginning. *Where does the circle begin? Where does it end? Which came first, the chicken or the egg?* **We think in straight lines, and the universe works circularly, rhythmically, undisturbed by our limited thinking.**

26) Our image of John has been drastically altered. He has become the *unmanifest* itself which is expressing itself as spirit, energy and matter. He is a spirit, eternal and unlimited. His expression, as that particular body which we see, is the unique thought formation caused by his previous experiences as an entity involved with matter. This thought formation condenses itself as an energy body and then as a physical body.

The basis of his reality is spiritual and atomic.

There are temporary changes going on in the formation of this mental, emotional and physical reality which we call John. These are *a passing show* which do not in any way affect his basic reality, which is like the unchanging projector light and the unchanging screen.

We unfortunately get all caught up in the play of emotional and mental images, and develop likes and dislikes, friends and enemies, loves and hates, attachments and aversions based on this illusory drama.

When we can change our focus from this changing emotional and mental melodrama to our spiritual and atomic unity, we will experience the basis of reality which is our oneness with John and all of creation.

«In truth we know nothing, for truth lies in the depths».

Dimocritos

CHAPTER VIII

COPING WITH THE DEPARTURE OF LOVED ONES

The emotions that we experience upon the death of a loved one or in any major loss such as divorce, loss of job or a part of the body have an intensity and power of their own. For this reason we are attending to this subject in a separate chapter.

Without a doubt, the most painful experience in life is the loss of a loved one. The most devastating for most people is the loss of a child or a spouse. Over the years, I have had the fortune to conduct seminars on death and immortality, and also support groups for those who have recently lost loved ones.

I am very grateful to all those who have attended and taught me by sharing their emotions, experiences and insights through the various stages of coping with this extremely painful and often totally overwhelming event.

In this chapter, I would like to share with you what I learned about coping with the death of loved ones throughout these years.

Note:

I repeat that I in no way underestimate the pain and strength of emotions we feel when we lose a loved one. This is **completely natural**. Please do not be offended when I encourage us all to let go and move on.

If you are not ready for some of the messages in this chapter or this book, that is perfectly natural. These emotions need time to dissipate. Come back to these pages again after some time; you may perceive them completely differently then.

EMOTIONS FREQUENTLY EXPERIENCED

Before discussing these emotions, I would like to clearly state that I respect the depth and strength with which such emotions can flood our being. Thus, when I point out other ways of looking at what is happening, it is not because I do not recognize the power of these emotions nor do I claim that we can easily change perspective. The fact, however, is that our evolutionary process demands that we begin to perceive ourselves, life and death in ways more aligned with the truth of our immortal nature. We need to transcend the limits created by our exclusive identification with our bodies and minds.

1. The **pain** of losing a loved one is similar to losing a part of our body. It hurts. We feel a part of our own selves is missing. It is simply inconceivable to us that our loved one simply does not exist anymore – in bodily form. We expect at any moment to hear or see him/her again.

What can we do? At first, there is not much that we can do but **simply observe, experience and express what we feel**. The more we allow ourselves to express this pain, the more quickly we can get through it.

We hurt. This is the truth. Nothing can alleviate this emotional pain except for a strong belief in the truths of life, and **even the Major Prophets have suffered great pains despite their unmatched faith**. If we do not already have this deep faith, it will be difficult for us to suddenly acquire it now. Thus, we are left with experiencing and expressing our pain.

We could find someone professionally trained to listen to, and facilitate our emotional expression and externalization. Meeting with him or her once a week can help us acknowledge and release our feelings. In addition to pain, we may feel fear, anger, guilt, jealousy, bitterness, etc. As we discuss each of these feelings, we need to acknowledge and accept them before they can pass on.

We can express them verbally, in written form, through movement or crying, or perhaps by emoting sounds or hitting a pillow. **It is best not hold back our tears or our pain at this point.**

In this way, the storm of emotions will pass much more quickly so we will be ready to accept what has happened and get on with our life.

In each case, there will be specific spiritual and emotional lessons or opportunities, but we cannot gain from these until we first discharge our emotions, pain, hurt and anger.

Once that is done, our loss becomes our gain. **Our pain becomes the triggering process that opens the door toward spiritual dimensions.** We now feel the need to learn the truth about life and ourselves; the truth that relieves all pain, all fear – Christ's Truth "which will set you free."

2. We can **fear** that we will not be able to continue living without the person whom we've lost. This applies especially to widows who have been programmed to believe they are weak and need a husband in order to be safe, secure or socially accepted. *It also applies to all situations in which we feel that we need that other person emotionally, physically, socially, mentally, economically or in any other way.*

The truth is that **losing a loved one is an excellent spiritual opportunity to develop our inner strength, security, worthiness and self-respect.** It may take some time to overcome the fear, but as it gradually subsides, we will be much stronger because of this loss. Each loss of external support is an opportunity to find inner strength.

3. We might feel **injustice** and **bitterness** that "Life" or God took our loved one. This is more intense when the departed one was young, a child or a spouse in the prime of life.

We cry, "WHY? Where is the justice? Why my child? Why my beloved spouse? Why has this happened to me? What have I done to deserve this? What did my loved one do to deserve this? What am I being punished for? I have done nothing to deserve this!"

Such an experience is obviously a very trying test of our faith in God and in the wisdom of Divine Justice. Many of us have lost our faith in and love for God in such moments. Remembering how Job and Abraham handled their tests may help us cultivate that faith which we are often lacking.

When we cry "WHY?" and rightly so, let us do it with all our might, demanding an answer! Then afterwards, let us then sit quietly alone with our eyes closed and **be willing to hear the response**. If we shout "WHY?" as an accusation, then we, in all fairness, must give the accused party the chance to answer and explain. Thus, after each "WHY?", let us sit quietly and be receptive, allowing our minds to be open so we may hear the answers. **There *are* answers if we want to hear them.** They may not come at the moment we are sitting. They may come after some time when we are watching a TV show, listening to the radio, talking with a friend, reading a book (perhaps this book), walking in nature, taking a bath, envisioning a dream, meditating, praying, or doing nothing at all.

They may come after many years, when our pain and anger have subsided enough to allow the truth to rise up from within. The truth is always there. We may not be ready to see it, because no one has ever helped us to be ready, because we live in a death-denying, non-believing society.

Thus, our loved one's death will eventually become an avenue toward greater understanding of the nature of reality and the laws of the universe. Our pain becomes a motivating force, pushing us toward the realization that **there is a perfect and just divine plan governing birth, death and all that is between**. We will then realize that our loved one's death was no accident, nor an injustice, but exactly what we both chose as souls in order to grow spiritually.

That does not mean that our loved one sacrificed his or her life so we could wake up spiritually. He or she got out of the "game of life" early and is the lucky one who had fewer lessons to take. We are staying, suffering and absorbing the lessons. What has happened was *perfect for our mutual evolution.*

We can believe this through faith and understanding the Universal Laws.

4. We might experience **depression** and **disillusionment** that life has no meaning without our loved one. This again is especially true when we have lost a child or spouse who was the "purpose of our lives", who was our main occupation.

We **identify with these roles** of parent, spouse or child and thus **learn to find our identity and meaning in life through them.** When the person or persons who played those roles with us suddenly disappears **we are left with depression unless we can find a new identity and meaning in life.**

This, of course, is a great spiritual opportunity in that we now have the chance to grow and evolve into new and hopefully more *universal roles.* We have found through the years that four basic goals help people to move forth with their lives more quickly.

First is the goal of **evolution** or self-improvement. Life is meaningful and interesting when we are working on improving ourselves.

The second is **creativity**. We experience joy when we create. Creativity can emerge in all areas of life from drawing, singing, dancing and writing to gardening, cooking, developing a business or bringing up children.

The third is **service**. We feel that our life has meaning when we can be of use to others, when we can make their lives happier or more comfortable in some way.

The fourth is **relationships**, which give our lives meaning, allow us to feel love, share and serve.

We encourage all persons to *align their lives* with these basic life purposes: evolution, creativity, service and relationship. This is especially important for persons who are in a state of depression.

5. We might feel **guilty** that we did not sufficiently express our love to that person. We might think, "I did not show him enough love. I scolded him too much. I complained too much. I was negative and unpleasant. I never told him how much I loved, respected and appreciated him. I was unpleasant and nagging."

All this may be true, although it is probably not as true as we now imagine it to be. Our loved one may not have experienced us as negatively as we imagine. If, however, we do harbor guilt, there are some solutions.

We can bring that person to mind and imagine that he or she is standing in front of us (this may require some practice in relaxation, positive projection, or meditation techniques). We can then communicate mentally with this person, expressing our remorse and regret, and ask for forgiveness (this can also be done in **written** form).

I did this with my Father who was murdered. It helped me overcome guilt I felt about not showing him the love and respect I always had for him.

We can also express our hurt, anger, disappointment and any other feelings. We can settle accounts. Our loved ones hear us, and thus, we can simultaneously forgive and ask forgiveness.

Such an exercise will bring us peace of mind. If we are accustomed to the sacraments of Confession and Holy Communion, we can partake in them as well.

Then let us forgive ourselves and be over with these **useless emotions of guilt** which do not help anyone at all – not our loved one and certainly not ourselves.

6. We might feel **guilty** thinking we could have done more to keep him or her alive. We might think, "I should have taken him to another doctor, to another hospital. If only we had done this other operation. If only I had been there when he died, I could have prevented it. *It is all my fault. I am to blame for his death.*"

Such feelings are common. Let us, however, take a closer look at them. Taking full responsibility for another's life or death is like playing God. Am I so godlike that I can keep someone alive? Such thoughts are totally in contradiction with the laws of the universe which state that each soul (in collaboration with his own self-created divine plan) decides the moment of physical birth and death. No one can create or prevent someone else's scheduled time of departure.

I do not believe that the person who shot my father was the cause of his death. I believe that he was *simply the means by which my father's death was manifested.* I believe that my father, as a soul, had chosen to die in this way on that day, although his conscious mind was totally unaware of this fact. The only thing he said after being shot, as he looked into the eyes of his assailant was, "WHY?"

Yet three days earlier, my mother heard him call out in his sleep, "Ray, Ray watch out he has a gun". Ray was the other professor who was shot by the same student five minutes earlier. The student shot Ray (whom my father was warning in his sleep) and then my father. My father *knew* in his subconscious mind that he would die on this day, but this remained unknown to his conscious mind.

If we believe in a divine law that dictates that each soul, in collaboration with the Divine, creates its own destiny, how can we believe that someone else is responsible for another's death, even he who pulls the trigger? Thus, how much more unreasonable it is for us to believe that someone died because we did not take him or her to one more doctor, do one more operation, or because we were not there when he or she left the body.

This, of course, does not mean that we should not do whatever we can to save every life. Nor does it mean that we allow those who harm or kill others exempt from justice. It is simply important to remember that when the soul departs, it has nothing to do with us or our presumed negligence. We are obliged to do whatever we can, but then we must offer our acceptance to the Divine all that results. As St. Paul declared, "not a hair moves on the head of man, without His will".

7. Some of us might experience **sorrow, disappointment, disillusionment and bitterness** that we do not have the emotional support we expected from friends and relatives. The days immediately after the funeral are filled with numerous mind-distracting activities. Many come to express their condolences. Perhaps they may offer various types of help. There are many official papers to be filled out, as well as many matters, economic and otherwise, to be addressed.

Then suddenly one day, all this passes and *we are alone perhaps for the first time* since our loved one departed. There are no more papers to fill out; no more matters to arrange.

Our friends have their lives to live, with their responsibilities, jobs, families and social engagements. They may feel uncomfortable in our presence, because they do not know what to say or do to help us feel better. They may even feel guilty that they still have their loved ones and are happy. Also, our pain might trigger their fear of losing loved ones, or their pain about the same or other matters.

As a result, they might not enjoy being with us, not because they do not love us or care for us, but *because they are unable to face the pain and suffering* which permeate our environment. This is especially so when we ourselves are obsessed with talking exclusively about the death of our loved one. The others may sit with us a number times, but eventually they will not be able to hear anymore about something *which they have no power to change.*

Such a situation may be an opportunity to cultivate understanding toward the others and their difficulties in the face of pain and suffering. It may be an opportunity to overcome the belief that we need others to feel well, to be happy or secure. We can overcome the belief that because we have passed through this terrible misfortune that others are obliged to pay attention to us and to help us, even if we ourselves are not ready to let go of our pain.

If we see people pulling away, **it may be that the time has come for us to release our pain and perhaps start helping others.** They, too, have their problems. **Loneliness can be healed by others reaching out to us or by our reaching out to them.**

Gradually, we will get on with our lives and connect with other people. Then our loneliness will disappear. Getting involved in **service toward others** who are lonely or need some type of selfless service will help considerably.

8. We may feel **loneliness**. We may think, "It is difficult to connect with other people. They are not open, not friendly. I have no one to talk to, to share with, to be myself with."

It is natural to feel lonely when we lose a loved one. We experience an emptiness which that person helped to fill. We have learned to fill our emptiness through others or through various stimuli such as TV, newspapers, stimulants, tranquilizers, and activities in general.

That which fills us *most*, however, is a **deep unconditional love relationship.** This is healing, supporting and verifying. It gives us a feeling of security and self-worth. It is natural to feel lonely when a person who offered us this love disappears, even if our relationship wasn't perfect.

Loneliness is the «dis- ease» of our times. It has nothing to do with *being alone*. We could be surrounded by many persons and feel lonely because we cannot be ourselves with them. Likewise, **we can be alone in seclusion and feel connected** with others, nature or the Divine.

If we can accept loneliness and face it, we might find that we can also feel well alone, or that we can feel comfortable and be ourselves with other persons who we do not know so well.

Another important aspect of **facing loneliness** is **developing a relationship with ourselves**. This we can do by actually *spending time alone* and learning to occupy ourselves and enjoy our solitary moments.

Focusing on our relationship with God through *prayer, meditation and other forms of awareness* of and communication with the Divine can also be very fulfilling.

Walks in nature can fill that emptiness as we feel our connection with the universe through nature.

And finally, by **serving others who are lonely** – the poor, the homeless, orphans and the elderly, **we fill our emptiness as we fill theirs**.

Remember: *our loneliness can disappear when others reach out to us, or when we reach out to them.*

9. We could likely feel jealous that others still have their loved ones and we do not. We have all felt jealousy when someone has something we do not have. Although **jealousy is natural**, *it will not bring our loved one back* and we often feel **guilty** about experiencing those emotions.

Accepting that we are jealous and perhaps allowing ourselves to **express it**, to confess it to someone we trust, **will help us release these feelings**.

It is amazing how our feelings gradually deflate when we confess them and share them with someone who can understand. This is an important phenomenon, that when we acknowledge our emotions and express them, they gradually dissipate.

We often do the *opposite*. We are afraid to admit our emotions *even to ourselves*. We fear that if we admit them to others, they will reject us. Such **suppression does not work** as others sense our emotions anyway.

This is true of all the emotions we are discussing in this section. We have *everything to gain* by recognizing them, admitting them and sharing them with someone who will understand. Also, our feelings will subside as we **get on with our lives** and learn to **enjoy** people and events, having nothing to envy in the others.

In addition, as we learn to believe in the **universal rule** that "*we are given exactly what we need in order to evolve and learn life's lessons*," we will be able to accept and be happy with what we have.

If we look objectively, we will see we are better off than a good 80% of our brothers and sisters on this planet.

10. It would be natural to feel **anger** toward those who were in some way connected with or "responsible for" our loved one's death. Perhaps a doctor made a mistake, or someone was driving recklessly, and now our loved one is dead.

Our pain demands that we find who committed this "wrong". Who has made this horrible mistake? Who is to blame? Feeling anger, in some cases, **serves to divert us from our pain and fear**.

This anger might also be directed toward God, who allowed this to happen, and may lead to *rejection* of God and all which has to do with Him. We think, "If there was a God, He would not have let this happen." We are angry and hurt.

In the case where some human was possibly at fault, we may even feel the need for *revenge*. We might want to make this person feel the same pain we feel. We think this might lessen our hurt. We cannot think clearly. We simply feel that someone must pay for what has happened here.

In such a case, we must find someone whom we trust to listen to us and acknowledge our feelings. We need help to see more objectively. We must be careful not to be carried away by the desire for revenge, for it will not remove our pain, nor make our loved one happy where he or she is. *For the truth is that no one was ultimately responsible for his or her death.* That moment and event were chosen by the soul which has left.

As for God, we have already mentioned that this is an opportunity to cultivate real faith. To stop believing in God because He did not do what we wanted Him to is like denying that a person exists because he or she refuses to give us something we ask from him or her.

Our children ask things from us which we choose not to give because we believe or know that it is best for them not to have those things at the present. Should they hate us for this or claim that we do not exist because we do not do what they want?

Our requests **are heard**, but often losing a loved one is so much *better* for our spiritual evolution and development, even though such a thought may bring even more pain and guilt. It is illogical to say that God does not exist simply because we do not understand what is best for our evolution and want things to remain as they always were in order for us to feel secure and happy.

11. We might also feel **anger** toward or **rejection** of our loved one who "chose" to leave the earth plane at this time, leaving us here alone. We may interpret this as a form of rejection, abandonment and *lack of love.*

We need to recognize, accept, admit and express all these **emotions**. We would do well to **seek help** in doing so. Then, we need to move on to the next step, which is to investigate and discover the specific **beliefs** that create our pain and other emotions.

We will then be ready to move on to study, believe and employ the **truth** in our lives. The truth is that we are immortal spirits that have temporarily incarnated in the material plane in order to continue our evolutionary process. We lose nothing by leaving. It is also *possible that we have agreed* that this would happen even before we incarnated into this material plane, that we agreed that he or she would leave and we would stay *so we both could learn our respective lessons.*

NEGATIVE THOUGHT FORMS

ABOUT THE DEATH OF A LOVED ONE

These emotions are the result of various beliefs, programmings or thought forms that have been instilled into our conscious and subconscious minds. As long as the beliefs are there, the emotions will come forth.

Let us look at some of these beliefs which generate these emotions within us.

1. I cannot live without him / her.

2. I am not secure without him / her.

3. No one else but he / she can give me joy or security.

4. My life has no meaning without him / her.

5. I want to die; I want to be with him / her.

We have been programmed to believe we must have specific persons close to us who will make us feel secure, happy, worthy, etc. **We give these persons the «keys» to our happiness and security.** Very likely, there was a time in our lives when we didn't even know them, when we were not with them. Now *we cannot imagine ourselves happy without them.*

The truth, however, is that we can. The fact that many **billions** of people have lost their loved ones in the past proves this. Each has struggled with these thoughts, but each has moved on to live a normal life when these feelings naturally subsided and the need to continue prevailed. We will eventually move on, just as all those before us have.

We will all lose everyone we know, either through our death or theirs. Each and every one of us will die within the next 70 to 90 years, some sooner, some later (taking into consideration the small children we know). We will lose everyone and they will lose us. **This is the nature of the physical universe.**

6. Death is a bad, painful experience.

This does not seem to be true. All who have died momentarily and returned report that leaving the body is a wonderful and very **enjoyable** experience. Very few actually wanted to return to the body. We who remain in life continue to suffer and learn lessons. Those who have left are on "vacation" from the school of life.

7. I don't have the right to be happy since my loved one has died.

8. I will betray my loved one if I allow myself to be happy.

9. I will betray my loved one if I love someone else as much as I loved him / her.

10. I will betray my loved one if I find a different purpose and meaning in my life.

Our loved ones are **immortal spiritual beings** who have played various roles with us in various life times in order that we all continue our evolution. Which loved one would we be betraying if we love another one from this life or the previous thousand lives? Have we not then betrayed all our loved ones from previous lives by loving those of this life?

How can love betray? Can love be promised to only one aspect of the Divine, or is it for all aspects of the Divine? I am not talking about sex or free sex, but about **love, service and unity.** *Can loving or serving another aspect of the Divine ever betray my loved one* who has moved on to another dimension? I would simply be **loving and serving another aspect of my loved one.**

11. I have been treated unjustly.

12. I am unlucky.

13. I am the most miserable person I know.

Every day, 40,000 parents are forced to witness their children's death, because they do not have the means to keep them alive. Yesterday 40,000 children. Today 40,000 children. Tomorrow 40,000 children. The day after tomorrow 40,000 children. This week 280,000 parents will see their children die. This month 1,112,000 parents will suffer their children's deaths. This year 13,440,000 parents will suffer their children's deaths. And next year? And in the 70 years of a normal life, 938,000,000 parents? Here we are not counting all the deaths of those other than children and those caused by wars, accidents, suicides, etc. Need I say more?

This may not soften our pain, but it should remove the false belief that we are unlucky, being treated unjustly or feel the most miserable. Yes, we have pain. No one can deny that, but we are not being treated differently than the rest of creation. *Life in the physical body is temporary.*

14. The other's death is a punishment for him or me.

15. I am a sinner; otherwise God would not have punished me in this manner.

16. God does not love me since He allowed my loved one to die.

17. There is no God; otherwise He would not have allowed my loved one to die.

My perception is that there is no punishment in the universe. There are only **lessons**. God is love. He gains no pleasure in punishing. We create our **evolutionary curriculum** in cooperation with the Divine. It is a shame that we interpret opportunities for growth as punishment.

If, as students, we decide to become doctors, we set ourselves up for a number of years of suffering in terms of expenses, limited freedom, and exhausting hours of study and examinations. We do not interpret these as punishment, for we remember that we have chosen this so as to develop the qualities we need in order to become doctors.

It the same way, we, as souls with the goal of manifesting our unlimited divine potential here on earth, program various tests and lessons through which we will be given the opportunity to develop those divine attributes. One of the most difficult, and yet most potentially liberating tests, is the loss of a loved one. It has nothing to do with punishment, neither for us nor for our loved one.

18. It is my fault he died. I could have done something more.

We have already mentioned that this thought is in direct violation of the Law of Creation. *We create our own physical birth and death. No one can do this for anyone except himself or herself.* If our time had not come, not even the greatest mass murderer in the world could have touched us. Everyone else would be touched except for those whose hour had not come. We are not in a position to change these events.

19. I did not have the chance to correct my relationship with him or her. I feel guilty. I was not entirely correct.

We can still correct this relationship by communicating with our loved one now. When we say communicate, we do not mean go to a medium and have a conversation with him or her. We do **not** recommend that this as a good idea. First of all, many «mediums» are not exactly what they say they are. Secondly, we may not be communicating with our loved one, but rather with some low-level spirit hovering around the earth rather than proceeding on in its evolution. Thirdly, **we hold our loved one back by such communications**. We call his or her attention toward the Earth level. It is a totally different thing to close our eyes and communicate with our loved one during those first days after his or her departure, **and totally another to badger him or her with mediumistic contacts for years after because of our inability to let go**.

We can close our eyes, bring our loved one into our awareness and express our feelings. We can forgive and ask for forgiveness, **then let go** and get on with our lives.

This can be done a few times in the beginning, and then after a few months if we notice that we still have suppressed feelings. **After a year or so, we would best let that soul get on with its work, and we with ours.**

20. He (she) deserted me. He (she) left me alone.

We do not choose death as a way of deserting another. *We have mutually chosen this event for our mutual spiritual benefit.*

Note:

I repeat that I in no way underestimate the pain and strength of emotions we feel when we lose a loved one. This is **completely natural**. Please do not be offended when I encourage us all to let go and move on.

If you are not ready for some of the messages in this chapter or this book, that is perfectly natural. These emotions need time to dissipate. Come back to these pages again after some time; you may perceive them completely differently then.

POSITIVE THOUGHT FORMS

There are some beliefs or thought forms, which can be very supportive in our effort to cope with the death of a loved one. If you find any of these helpful, write them down with large letters and place them where you can see them often. Feel free to alter them to apply more appropriately to your own specific needs.

You could also make a record with these messages to play while in deep relaxation or as you fall asleep.

1. I am an eternal soul and have the power to live an abundant and meaningful life. All is within me.

2. My loved one is an eternal, immortal soul who continues to live in another dimension more beautiful than the one in which I currently exist.

3. Since my loved one is very well and far closer to his or her true nature and to God, I can be glad for him / her and can give joy to myself and to those around me.

4. God is within and around me, so I always feel secure, protected and tranquil.

5. Everything happens according to a perfect and just Divine Plan that gives to each of us what he or she needs for our soul's evolution. For some reason, it was best for my loved one to move on to another level of existence. As for my own evolution toward God, it is best that I continue on here, even without him or her.

6. Everyone on this earth has lost loved ones (not only me). Also, we will all eventually lose all the people we know because we are only temporarily on this earth and our departure is perfectly natural.

7. The departure of the soul from the restrictions of the temporary physical body is a beautiful liberation from a very limited incarnated state.

8. The loss of my loved one is a great opportunity for spiritual development through the cultivation of inner power, tranquility, security and self-acceptance.

9. I accept the perfection of the Divine Plan, and I forgive God and everyone for what is happening to me. I release all for any responsibility for my reality.

10. My loved one would want me to be happy and to continue my life creatively and beautifully.

11. I am acceptable, lovable, and interesting because of what I am, not because of my relationship with someone.

12. The loss of a loved one is not related to punishment, but is instead a great opportunity for spiritual development and inner growth.

13. I am a pure child of God and He loves me unconditionally.

14. No one can be responsible for someone else's death. Each person has selected the hour and the place when he or she will leave. Other people or situations are simply the instruments we use for our departure.

15. I can, even now, correct my relationship with my loved one with inner concentration and prayer.

16. We are all evolving souls, all children of God. I open myself to my brothers in the family of humanity who are now with me on this planet. My loved one would want me to do so.

17. I share with others my sorrow and joy. We are one big family of humanity.

18. I find meaning in life by serving, creating and evolving. This is why I have come on this Earth.

19. Life is a gift of God, and it is my duty to use it for my benefit and that of others.

20. Today, 40.000 parents have lost their children. Tomorrow, another 40.000 parents will lose their children. I am not alone in pain. The soul's departure from the physical body is a natural part of life on earth.

21. There is only one universal life force, which expresses itself through all beings. The same consciousness that expressed itself through my loved one is now expressing itself through everyone around me. Loving and offering to others, I love and offer to him / her.

STEPS WE CAN TAKE

1. We can **study the spiritual truths** related to the following topics:

> **a.** What is a human being?
>
> **b.** What is the relationship between the soul and the body?
>
> **c.** Why does a soul take on a body?
>
> **d.** What happens when the soul leaves the body?
>
> **e.** What is the relationship between man, nature and God?

2. We can **express our feelings openly** to those who can respect and understand them, even if that means finding a "professional listener" (Perhaps a priest, minister, psychologist, spiritual teacher or a good friend).

3. We can **pray for our loved ones' development** and growth as souls on the dimensions where they are now residing. We can light a candle for them as frequently as we feel the need, sending them energy and love.

We do not need to go to the grave. Our loved ones are not there. During the first days, they are most likely wherever we are. *They are not attracted to the discarded body, but to those they love.* We can ask others to pray for them also. This is important for the **first forty days and then less so for another year**.

4. We can gradually free ourselves from excessive concentration on those who have left this plane and **pay more attention to those who are here** with us. It might be best eventually to remove belongings that remind us of him or her. We can give them to charity or to those who need them or would appreciate them. Their presence around the home will obstruct our gradual detachment and the ability to move forward with our lives (which is what our loved ones would want).

5. We can occupy ourselves with meaningful activities four of which are:

     a. Service

     b. Creativity

     c. Evolution - Self knowledge

     d. Conscious Love Relationships

6. We need to **be patient with ourselves** and those around us. Overcoming such a shock will usually take time.

7. We can **cultivate faith in God** and in ourselves.

8. We can **join a group of people** dedicated to the process of growth where we can mutually support each other in this process.

Books by the same author which deal with this subject are:

     a) *"The Mystical Circle of Life"*

     b) *"Universal Philosophy"*

     c) *"Miracles of Love and Wisdom"*

CHAPTER IX

THE EVOLUTION
OF A SQUIRREL

A Modern Myth

It was exactly 21 minutes before midnight.
The sky was very dark; no moon,
not even a star.
I was lying at the bottom of the largest tree
I had ever seen. In fact, the branches
reached up so high in the sky
that I couldn't see the top.
I was there, not by accident -
for coincidence
is a word we use to explain those events
which follow laws we
have not yet discovered.

I was there to hear the life of «Who Owl», who had been sitting
immovably continuously, and silently for the last twelve years.
If fact, it will be exactly 12 years at midnight.
How did I know that he would break
his silence at 21 minutes to midnight?
I just happened to be here by design.

It began.
Whuuuuuuuuuuuuuuuuuuuuuuuuuuuuu
with my eyes closed
 the sound began creating images in my mind and the story began
to unravel like a dream
in color and   sound   which came from every where
uuuuuuuuuuuuuuuuuuuuu.

«Whuuuuuuuu... it was 84 years ago at midnight that the sun confused the world by coming out at night. But even the sun can get bored with such routine, coming out only during the day.

«A brilliant beam of light flashed down to earth at the root of this tree. The light solidified into an egg, a snake's egg.

«Whuuuuuuuuuuuuuuuuu... that was my beginning on the earth. I emerged as a snake and made my home in the first hole of this tree, on the ground level. I never looked up. I crawled in two dimensions only. Only two things interested me during those twelve years – **food** and **sleep**. I moved only as necessary to have food. I would kill my food, eat it, and lie in the sun to digest. This was the extent of my life.

«Each winter brought hibernation and shedding of skin, and each spring was a rebirth into a new skin. But all was the same: new skin, same me. Searching food and sleeping.

«Whuuuuuuuuuuuuuuu... in the 13th year I awoke in the second hole of the tree. I was transformed. I was now a squirrel with four legs and a much shorter tail. But I had no memory of my previous snakehood. The instinctual need for food and sleep remained, but a new desire was searching for fulfillment within me. I wanted a mate and family.

«I left my hole searching only for a mate, or food for myself and my family. Each winter brought hibernation, and each spring rebirth. Each spring was a clean new start, for when I awoke I had no memory of the previous year or of my previous family.

«These were not easy years, for although I desired to have a mate, it was nearly impossible to live in harmony with them. I had to learn responsibility and compromise, which are not so easy as one might think.

«But each spring I awoke with a fresh desire to try it all again, a new mate, a new family. Now don't get the idea that it was all troubles – there were many beautiful moments of togetherness and love.

«For twelve years, with twelve mates and twelve families I lived in the second hole of this eternal tree.

«Whuuuuuuuuuuuuuuuu... in the 25th year I found myself in the third hole of the tree. I looked down to see a world out there full of squirrels and other animals. Although I had no recollection of my 24 years in the lower holes, the instinctual need for food, sleep, a mate and family remained.

«In addition, however, I now had the ambition to make something of myself in the world. I had desire for power, money, fame and social achievement. I achieved these goals to varying degrees during the 12 summers spent in this hole of the tree.

«During the first summer I became a famous athlete. I was well known on all the lower holes of the tree.

«However, winter came and with it, dreaded hibernation. I had really come to fear and wanted to avoid this inevitable hibernation. It meant an end to all the power, professions, and fame I had accumulated and become attached to during the summer.

«The next spring I awoke with a gift for buying and selling. During that next year I became an extremely wealthy merchant and I indulged in every luxury for myself and my family. It was perhaps during the approach of winter that year that I had the greatest fear of hibernation. All my wealth would dissolve in the rain of time separating winter from spring.

«During my third summer there I became a teacher of young squirrels. In the 4th I was ill much of the time and took odd jobs at home. The remaining summers in the third hole found me mastering various careers: a famous actor, a drama critic, a lawyer, a thief, an explorer, a powerful politician, a revolutionary guerrilla, and my last summer was spent as a social worker.

«Whuuuuuuuuuuuu... I awoke in the 37th year of my life on the fourth level, once again ignorant of my years on the lower levels. Food, sleep, a mate, a family, power, money, fame, all continued to be a part of what interested me, but new strange urges were growing within me.

«There was a need for love and communication with others. I began joining together with other groups of squirrels and other animals on the fourth level. I was trying somehow to be open and loving towards all beings, even if they weren't squirrels.

«We joined together according to various interests, whether it be games or business, pleasure or work. It was just an excuse to be together and share ideas, feelings and love.

«My family was still an important part of my life during those early years on this level, but toward the 44th year my interest was projected more outward. I was interested in helping society in some way, Then in the summer of my 44th year I first came in contact with a "**BORING Group**".

«I had heard the word before, but had always been conditioned by the slogan so predominant on the lower levels, "Boring is boring". (As a noun the first "boring" indicates the act of drilling a hole into the center of the tree for upward passage. As an adjective the second "boring" shows it 's pretty dull).

«There was a magnetic atmosphere of peace and love in the room, and all the other squirrels accepted me with a gentle smile. In the front, about to speak was a very special white-haired squirrel with the shortest tail I had ever seen. And even more to my amazement he had a few owl feathers sticking out of his side.

«My friend, who had brought me, understood my amazement and explained that this squirrel had come down from the fifth level and that many of the squirrels on that level had begun to grow feathers.

«That was also the first time I was aware consciously of the fact that this tree actually had six holes or seven levels on which one could live.

«As the wise old squirrel spoke it was as if he were picking knowledge and truth out of my own mind and placing it before my eyes so that I could see it more clearly.

«I didn't really remember much of the details of what he said, but I was so overwhelmed by his love and peacefulness and understanding that, I began to attend these "Boring meetings" more and more regularly.

«We talked, sang, danced, and ate together, but in a different way than in the 3rd hole where all was competition and aggression. I spent less and less time in the lower holes and became more and more absorbed in these groups.

«We started therapy clinics and welfare centers for the less fortunate animals. In general we were concerned for the welfare of the whole animal community --not just our own individual needs.

«Twelve years, I lived in this way. Toward the end I was less fearful of hibernation, thanks to the "Boring meetings" through which we learned that although we lost all our possessions and family during the hibernation period, the important fact was that we were the same consciousness which woke up the following spring.

«We learned certain habits of living by which we could be happier and more loving squirrels. By obeying these laws of nature our tails grew steadily shorter, and, theoretically, one day we would begin to grow feathers and stand on two legs like the wise squirrel from the fifth level.

«Deep inside every squirrel wanted to fly, but very few really believed they ever would. The laws of nature which we were to follow in order to prepare our bodies and minds for flying someday to the infinitely distant top of the tree in which we lived were:

1) Not to harm ourselves or any other being in the forest.
2) Never to lie or deceive ourselves or others.
3) Never to take anything which was not rightfully ours.
4) Never to take or want more of anything than what we needed for a simple squirrel life.

5) To treat all other beings, no matter what their form, as we would like to be treated ourselves.
6) To be content with our present condition while always trying to improve.
7) To practice daily cleansing of our bodies and thoughts.

«These guidelines for living constituted the foundation for safe and successful "Boring" as the inner need of every squirrel's life, whether he knew it or not.

«So on faith and belief in what the elder Squirrels told us, I tried as well as I could to follow these suggestions from my 44th to my 49th year. I often failed and had many moments of doubt and confusion as to whether it was worth it. Occasionally I would sneak down to the 3rd hole in the evening and enjoy nightly squirrel pleasures. But the morning after I was always full of guilt and vowed to never again abuse myself in that way.

«This often renewed my determination to find the inner strength to follow the 7 laws of nature and attend more "Boring meetings".

«*Whuuuuuuuuuuuu...* » *the wise old "Who Owl" continued his unbroken Whuuu.*
This was all in one breath, mind you,
and it was now 9 minutes to midnight.
But very strangely it was
becoming lighter in the sky.
The Whuuu... carried me back to the story.

«Whuuuuuuuuuuu... In my 49th spring I awoke with a very joyous feeling in my heart. I was a lighter colored squirrel and had a rather shorter tail. And I soon discovered that I was living on the fifth level of this endlessly ancient tree.

«The instinctual, natural desires of my earlier years as a snake and a squirrel living in the lower holes had been greatly attenuated by the repeated observance of the 7 laws of nature.

«I had a simple love in my heart for all beings, and during these years I took a family or profession or not, as was most suitable for my one main purpose – understanding the truth about life.

«I spent the first few summers studying at the higher level universities and centers for learning on this 5th level. Here we learned the laws of physical nature, and this we called science. I mastered completely the knowledge of physical nature, and became in a short time the foremost authority on methods of climbing to the infinitely high top of the tree in which we all live.

«This was always the unspoken goal of every squirrel scientist: to devise a way to ascend to the unreachable top-limit of our known world.

«Others working on a more mystical level conceived the idea that squirrels could fly. And indeed there were some flying squirrels, but unfortunately they could only fly laterally or downward.

«Although I was the most renowned scientist in my field, I began to become quite disillusioned with my work and the approach. I had become so involved in my feverish attempt to solve this problem with all the facts known to squirrels at that time, that I lost all contact with the love and happiness with which I had begun my years on the fifth level. I had even given up observing the 7 laws.

«I had begun to seriously wonder what life was all about – Why was I alive? Why was I a squirrel and not some other animal? Why was I this particular squirrel and not some other squirrel? Everything seemed meaningless and confused. There seemed to be no purpose in life, not even the 7 laws, or "Boring groups" (which truly, now, were boring). Science had failed me. I had come to the end of the trail. I didn't care to live anymore. There was no purpose, no reason to live.

«I decided to jump out of the fifth level and end my life in the perilous fall to the ground.

«I stood ready and determined to take that final and fatal step, to put an end to my tormented mind.

«But here as I was standing looking down, ready to jump, I saw far far below a snake crawling along the earth toward the first hole of the tree. And before I could really understand the strange feeling which that sight created within me, I heard for the very first time the eerie sound of the «Whuuuuuuuu» from far above. In the sky far above the fifth level, I saw the spectacular flight of what I now know to be an owl.

«The snake below, the owl above and the "Whuuuuuu" released some great tension in my mind, and a flood of strange feelings and ideas began to flow into my body and mind. It was like a river flowing after the first autumn rain, soothing and healing the thirsty riverbed dried and cracked by the scorching summer sun.

«I turned and walked in a trance-like state toward my 5th level abode, contemplating that strange sight of the owl and snake and the feeling it created within me.

«Upon arriving home, to my great surprise I found the door open and inside was sitting an elderly squirrel, white-haired and with a few feathers on his back side. Immediately the memory of my earlier years with the "Boring groups" came back to me. This was my first "past-summer recall", as I was soon to learn to call them.

«Somehow and in some strange way I half expected this squirrel to be there and also I intuitively knew that I was supposed to sit in front of him and that he was going to speak to me. As he spoke, it was like my earlier "Boring meeting" experiences, where the speaker seemed to be picking the thoughts out of my own mind and simply putting them into words before me so that I could clearly see them. They were ideas that were seeds within me – he was ripening them so that I could eat and digest them.

«He began and I listened:

«"You have seen the snake and the owl. The snake is your past. The owl is your destined future. The snake egg was formed from a beam of light, and the egg hatched the snake; that was your beginning in this tree. For 12 years you lived like a snake according to the desires of a snake, ignorant of the beam of light from which you originated, and which continues to be the only source of your life. This light is the thread linking together your summers which are only apparently broken by the hibernation in winter.

«"You have spent 42 years as a squirrel, also ignorant of your essential "light nature", and of your destiny to reunite with that nature. You are in a process of evolution. You will develop into an owl gradually over the years, and then you will be transformed into the beam of light which you really are, have always been, and always will be.

«"This is the purpose of life – to realize your light nature. There is a method of doing this, and you shall learn it. We call it **Boring.** Not as you know "boring" from your previous group meetings, although that has prepared you to take this step now.

«"You have sought to reach the limitless heights of this tree through all of your facts and formulas.

«"Well, here is a fact you know, but have ignored. It is impossible to scale this tree from the outside, because every winter all is wiped clean. Even if you could extend summer for an immeasurable amount of time (and may the sun forbid such a thing) you could not succeed because the law of gravity prevents any gross physical matter from reaching those heights. This is a law of nature.

«"Only energy – light energy can reach the top of the tree".

«At this point I interrupted my teacher, and, trying to impress him with my own ability to think for myself, asked, "But what about that owl I saw flying so high in the sky? How can **his** body go so high?"

«He smiled compassionately and calmly answered as if it were the next thing he was going to say. "But it is possible to raise the energy level of the molecules of your squirrel body and this manifests as the gradual replacement of fur with feathers. The tail, which is the extent of your lower nature, decreases, along with a decrease in the density of the molecules of your physical body. The feathers symbolize evolved consciousness and increased energy in your physical form".

«Now my mind was racing – it all made sense and I was eager to undergo this process. I was excited – life had meaning, life had purpose. And I had a grand destiny ahead of me. "How do I do this?" I asked.

«Before I could understand what was happening, his eyes were closed and his mouth opened into a perfect circle. With a deep, full breath, he gently but ever so powerfully exhaled the sound, " Whuuuuuuuuuuuuuuuuuuu..."

«I understood that I was to join him. At first my attempts were very weak and self-conscious, and then rather loud and boisterous. Finally, when I gave up trying, it was as if the sound of his "Whuuuuu..." entered into my heart, and my heart began to vibrate according to the law of sympathetic vibration in harmony with his. Without effort at all, as if I didn't exist, the Whuuuu began to flow from my heart. There was no longer "his Whuuu", and "my Whuuu", there was only one Whuuuuu flowing of its own accord through our united hearts.

«When the Whuuuuu subsided on its own, it continued on a mental level and my lesson continued silently. We both sat with our spines straight, eyes closed, hearts and minds in total union, and the answer to my question began to flow up from the depths of our united mind:

«"In the center of this tree there lies a central channel of subtle matter called the "sushumna canal". This is an exact replica of a similar channel which lies in the center of your spinal column. This channel of soft, highly energized material which cannot be detected by the scientific instruments of today but shall be in the future, connects the six holes or levels of this tree including the 7th level which is the top. The bottom three are called "holes" for those who live in them truly live in darkness. From the fourth to the sixth they are called "levels" for here begins the conscious awakening. There is no name for the limitless top, for no words can describe it.

«"And within you are six centers of energy plus the top level. You are undergoing 12-year cycles of awakening these centers within you while living on each level of the tree. As this process takes place, the molecules of your body and mind are energized and infused with greater and greater consciousness.

«"**Boring** is the method of clearing out the central canal within the tree so that you may rise to higher levels of the tree. Until now this has happened automatically and unconsciously, especially during periods of sleep and hibernation when your **light nature** attended to the task. But now you must do this **consciously**, so as to infuse also the conscious mind with this light nature.

«"This is done by boring in your own spinal column and awakening the centers of consciousness within yourself. As you transform your inner reality, so will your outer reality change.

«"This is done by boring the mind with the question WHOOOOOO? Which sounds like Whuuuuuuu..., the sound made by the great owls. It symbolizes the question WHO AM I?

«"Whuuuu is the sound the Light makes when it forms the snake's egg. Whuuu is the sound of the Light while it sustains your life. Whuuu is the sound the Light makes when the Owl is transformed back into Light and merges back into the Sun. Whuuu is the thread which connects all beings living in this great tree.

«"Make the sound of the Whuuu in your mind constantly, and especially at the point of falling asleep for winter hibernation. Whuuuuuuuuuuuuuuuu".

«I opened my eyes and he was gone, but I felt his presence within me. We were merged on some deep level forever.

«I spent the next seven years practicing the various disciplines of eating, breathing, exercising, and boring as instructed by the many teachers and books which came my way – always at the right time and in the right place.

«The seven laws had become my very nature, and I spent these seven years rather isolated from society in the incessant search for the answer to the question "Who am I?"

«All answers seemed to be within me, but often needed external beings or experiences to draw that understanding forth. It was rather difficult; a time of testing, and there were occasional moments of confusion, doubt, and wanting to give it all up.

«There were times when I felt that nothing had changed and that no progress had been made. But something from inside wouldn't let me stop. That wise old squirrel with the feathers was always speaking to me from my heart.

«He would leave me alone to flounder in my confusion until I was at the point of desperation. Only then would he intercede with his miraculous hand to give me a boost or restore my faith. It was always a terrible test, but nothing else seemed important now.

«Whuuuuuuuuuuuuu... it was my 61st year when I first awoke on the 6th level. I had my first feathers. I was excited at first, but after a while it seemed quite normal. Along with the diminishing tail and increasing feathers came other mental and physical powers.

«I was soon able to recall at will experiences of past summers, all the way back to my days as a snake on the first level. I could also do this for other squirrels, but avoided it unless absolutely necessary.

«A peaceful, powerful magnetism began to develop within and around me. Others came to absorb these vibrations. When necessary, and within the law of recycle, I would lay my hands on the ill or the unhappy to relieve them. I would teach and repeat various sounds and phrases which called upon beneficial forces known only to those living on the sixth level.

«At every moment, however, my mind was engaged in the Whuuuu which had become a continuous river of energy, love, and consciousness flowing through my heart. No matter what I was doing, saying or thinking, the Whuuu was the ether upon which these actions moved, just as water supports a boat.

«I had become a channel, a receiver of cosmic energies which descended from the limitless above and were transformed into deeds, words and thoughts through the medium of material body and mind.

«I offered all thoughts, words and actions to the Sun, to the light which was my very nature, and to the wise "Who Owls" who sat silently on the limitless top of the tree, offering silent inspiration to all who could open themselves to receive.

«During the last six years on the 6th level, I taught to those who would hear.

«I taught the law of recycle, which operates on so many levels and which is so essential to be made conscious for the squirrel interested in boring to the truth.

«The law of recycle, also called the "law of return" or "law of cause and effect", is demonstrated by the complete circle of molecules from the roots of the tree to the fruit of the tree. The fruit is eaten by the squirrel which then digests it and eliminates it from his body, allowing it to fall to the roots of the tree where it begins its return journey back to the fruit and the squirrel.

«Each squirrel must realize that this is so with every thought, word and action which is sent out. It ultimately returns as fruit which must be eaten, like it or not. Everything returns.

«This also is true of consciousness. Consciousness leaves the body during sleep and returns upon waking. Consciousness leaves the body during hibernation and returns with a new body for the next spring. That new body is also the fruit of the sum total of thoughts, words and actions of all the previous summers, beginning with the emergence of the snake from the egg.

«All squirrels must seek to liberate themselves from the law of recycle in order to actualize their manifest destiny as owls and finally as the Divine light.

«Squirrels can progress in this evolutionary process in the 7 following ways:

1) By observing the 7 laws of nature.
2) By giving up all desire for the fruit of their actions.
3) By working for the good of all beings without selfish desires.
4) By being devoted to the qualities of Truth, Love, Peace and Righteousness, and to those beings who manifest these qualities.
5) By studying the Truth as silently communicated by the "Who Owls".
6) By incessant practice of Boring with the Whuuuuuuuuuuuuuuuu (along with the preparatory exercises which lead to proper Boring).
7) By an act of the Divine SUN which liberates one Owl every 84 years.

«I taught with love, compassion and detachment. I expressed equal love for all and saw all beings as my self. No longer was I blinded by their physical form, but I looked deep within them, seeing the divine light which was my very own nature.

«I was no longer separate from the universe, but I lived immersed in the sea of the one light which expressed itself as my body and as all the other objects of the universe.

«Bliss was my very nature, although I manifested other emotions for the others' sake.

«Whuuuuuuuuuuuuuuuuuuu... the time was coming for the final metamorphosis. The hormones of my squirrel body had been completely altered in chemistry. My tiny tail was there only for its own sake, and I was completely covered with feathers.

«On the hibernation eve of my 72nd year, I called together my closest disciples and informed them that the time of my final hibernation had come.

«They rejoiced, and I gave my last discourse. "Each of them fell immediately into trance and received whatever they needed to hear.

«Whuuuuuuuuuuuuuuuu... in the spring of my 73rd year I awoke as a "Who Owl" and sat completely motionless on the limitless limit for 12 years, in total mental silence, allowing pure consciousness to flow through my emptiness down into the tree.

«And at this moment twelve years are complete...

Whuuuuuuuuuuuuuuuuuuuuuuuuuuuuuuuuuuuuuuuuuuuuuuuuuuuuuuu uuuuuuuuuuuuuuuu».

Suddenly the Whuuu became tremendously loud and all the forest shook.
My eyes opened suddenly but only to be blinded by the dazzling Sun,
shining in the midnight sky.

For a moment I caught sight of the
"Who Owl",
but only to see him evaporate into pure light which beamed back into the Sun,
absorbing the thunderous Huuuu with it.

Then, Silence and Darkness.

CHAPTER X

QUESTIONNAIRES ON THE ACCEPTANCE OF DEATH

It is now time to discover and analyze your own feelings and thoughts about life and death. The information in this book is *useless* unless **we can begin to employ it in our lives.**

Answering the following questions will help you to discover which beliefs, addictions, or fears are preventing you from being able to accept your own death or the death of your loved ones.

The same obstacles which prevent us from being able to accept death prevent us from being able to accept the flow of life itself. Life is a series of small deaths of all our attachments. Working on understanding these blockages, will help us to live our lives more fully, more happily and more in harmony with our inner values.

The following questions will help you to discover, objectify and transcend the various fears, attachments and emotional blockages which cause you to fear death, and of course, life itself.

Look deeply into yourself for the answers. In freeing yourself from these blockages you will experience more energy, love and joy in life.

HOW DO YOU IMAGINE YOUR
DEPARTURE FROM YOUR PHYSICAL BODY?

1. How do you imagine it will be when you leave your physical body?

_____
_____
_____
_____
_____
_____

2. Are you afraid of this process? If yes, what are you most afraid of concerning your leaving the body? Write here whatever fears you can think of.

_____
_____
_____
_____
_____
_____

3. Which truths or beliefs would you like to strengthen in order to face our own departure more peacefully and perhaps even joyfully?

_____
_____
_____
_____
_____
_____

4. What would you have liked to have done or completed concerning others, your work, or in general concerning your life in order to feel more ready and more comfortable in leaving your body?

_____
_____
_____
_____

LEAVING THE MATERIAL WORLD BEHIND

1. Imagine that you are about to leave your physical body and that you will not be returning to this particular body or personality. What will you miss most in leaving? (Do not include loved ones – we will work with them later.)

Think of the following:

a) Material objects and your belongings in general

b. Homes, buildings, lands etc.

c) Sensual pleasures (food, sex, movies, any sensual stimulus, nature)

d) Ambitions, goals, objectives, plans

e) Professional position or professional activities

f) Ideas and philosophies

g) Aspects of your personality

h) Talents and abilities

i) Other (we will work with relationships later)

2. What **three things will you miss most** when you have to leave the physical world?

_____
_____

3. What are the **beliefs** which you would like to strengthen in order to be able to leave the physical realm more easily and with the least negative feelings?

_____
_____

DECLARE HERE YOUR LAST WILL AND TESTAMENT

What would you like to happen with the material possessions which you are leaving behind?

_____
_____
_____
_____
_____
_____
_____
_____
_____
_____
_____
_____
_____
_____
_____
_____
_____
_____
_____
_____
_____
_____
_____
_____
_____
_____
_____
_____
_____

PURIFYING OUR CHARACTER

1. When you leave your physical body you will be taking with you your character, all of your tendencies, positive and negative. You will then experience an after death state or "environment" which will depend on the purity of your character and your mental and emotional tendencies. Also, in your next life you will continue with the same basic character traits. Which aspects of your character would you like to improve before leaving? Consider your fears, attachments, habits, weaknesses, attitudes and behaviors.

_____

_____

2. Which beliefs would you like to strengthen in order to make those improvements in your character?

_____

_____

_____

_____

3. Write here the truth which you would most like to strengthen.

_____

_____

4. Describe here how you would like your personality to be ideally:

_____

_____

_____

_____

_____

_____

_____

_____

_____

_____

_____

_____

_____

PEACE WITH OUR CONSCIENCE

Note here some of your behaviors, thoughts, words, actions or attitudes which are occasionally out of alignment with your conscience (you might feel shame or guilt or your actions may not express as much love, peace, respect, unity or selflessness as you would like). This could include what you do and also what you do not do.

1. _____
2. _____
3. _____

A. Analysis of **first behavior**, which is:

_____

1. The **feelings** and or **needs** which move you toward this behavior are (consider emotions such as fear, injustice, anger, disappointment, feeling betrayed, guilt, shame self doubt, self rejection and various needs such as to protect your self worth, security, freedom, various pleasures, etc.):

_____

2. The **beliefs** which create in you the above mentioned feelings and needs are (consider especially defense mechanisms such as beliefs which cause you to feel that your safety, self worth, or freedom to satisfy your needs are in danger):

1. _____
2. _____
3. _____

3. The **opposite positive beliefs** or **spiritual truths** which will free you from these false perceptions and maintain a behavior of love, peace and respect towards yourself and others are:

1. _____
2. _____
3. _____
A. Analysis of **second behavior**, which is:_____

Same process as above:
QUESTIONS WHICH HELP US

CONNECTING WITH OUR INNER GUIDANCE

1. When you were a child the things (activities, hobbies, interests, ideals) which were **most important to you** at various ages were:
a. before 9 years old   **b.** between 9 and 12   **c.** 13 to 15   **d.** 15 to 18
e. 19 to 21   **f.** 21 to 25

2. If you were told that you would die in 5 years, and that you would be healthy and active until that moment, how would you live your life?
         a. family   **b.** work   **c.** personal time

3. If you had to give **three messages** to the people of the world which for you were the most important guidelines for them to live by, what would they be?

4. If you had **three wishes** from a genie, who could give you special powers, what powers would you ask for:
         a. If they were for your self?
         b. If they were to be used for others?

5. Describe here exactly **how you would like your life to be** if there were **no limitations** whatsoever. Remember to describe all aspects of your life: physical, mental, social, professional, family, personal, spiritual, etc.

6. If your children asked you why we live, why we are on this planet, what is the purpose of life, **what should be their goals in this life** – how would you answer them?

7. What are your **talents**, and **abilities** which come naturally to you, which are inherent in your personality?

8. When are the **moments** or in which **situations have you felt the greatest satisfaction,** fulfillment or sense of comfort with your self and the world around you?

9. What kinds of **activities or situations bring you the greatest joy?**

10. What is it that you think you are **best equipped to offer** to others?

11. What **talents, abilities or character traits** would you like to **develop** further at this point in your life?

12. If in fact you are an **instrument** of a higher universal power (consciousness) which is governing all activities on the earth, seeking to manifest its latent potential in physical reality, and through all beings as physical instruments of its expression – what could be the **roles** which you (as one of those physical instruments) have **incarnated to play** in the cosmic drama?

ALIGNMENT WITH YOUR LIFE PURPOSE

1. What are your goals and ambitions? What would you like to accomplish in your life before leaving your physical body. Consider the following and other goals.

a) Personal goals

_____

_____

b) Family goals

_____

_____

g) Professional and economic goals

_____

_____

d) Social objectives

_____

_____

e) Spiritual goals

_____

_____

f) Other goals

_____

_____

2. If you knew that you would be leaving your body in **10 years** would you live differently than you do now? Which activities would you probably initiate or increase and which would you decrease or cease completely?

Initiate / increase _____

Decrease / Cease _____

3. If you knew that you would be leaving your body in **2 years** would you live differently than you do now? Which activities would you probably initiate or increase and which would you decrease or cease completely?

Initiate / increase _____

Decrease / Cease _____

OBSTACLES TOWARD THE FULFILMENT
OF THE PURPOSE OF LIFE

A. Which changes or moves you would like to make so as to be more in accord with the purpose of your life?

1.

2.

3.

4.

B. In connection with these changes, think if there are the following obstacles:

1. Are you concerned about what the others will think?

a) Who?

b) What do you believe they will think?

c) Why do you mind that they will have these thoughts?

2. Do you have some financial insecurity in connection with these changes? What do you believe?

3. Do you have attachments to some comforts which stop you from living your life more in accord with your purposes?

a) What comforts?

b) What will you miss if you don't have them?

4. Do you have attachments to exterior sources of security, enjoyment or affirmation which stop you from moving onwards your life purposes?

a) What are these attachments?

b) What will happen if you don't have them?

5. Is the fear or doubt that you won't succeed to do, or complete what you want to do, an obstacle?

6. Do you lack self-control and will power? If so, what can you do about it?

7. Do you perhaps have lack of faith to God, to the soul or to spiritual life? If so, what can you do about it?

8. Do you perhaps believe that you are too old for changes and that you have missed the opportunities for change?

9. Do you have conflict of needs?
Note here some of the conflicts:

One part of the self wants to doesn't	**But another part**
a.	
b.	
c.	
d.	

C. Now make a plan relating to how you will overcome the probable obstacles to the fulfillment of your life's purposes.

FORGIVENESS AND FREEDOM

1. Are there persons you would find difficult to be separated from either because of your or their departure from the physical body? Who? For each person, list a few reasons why you would find it difficult to accept their leaving their body (what is it that you would lose by losing the physical presence of this temporary manifestation of an immortal spirit? What will being missing from your life?)

a_____

_____

b_____

_____

c_____

_____

2. Are there persons towards whom, if you were now separated by your or their departure from the physical body, you would feel some type of guilt or remorse because you have not yet expressed something to them or done something for them which you would like to? What is that you would like to express to them or do for these persons before you or they eventually depart?

a_____

_____

b_____

_____

c_____

_____

3. Are there persons you have the need to forgive before you depart from each other? Who and for what do you need to forgive them ?

a_____

_____

b_____

_____

c_____

_____

4. Are there persons you would like to ask forgiveness from before you depart from each other? Who and for what do you need to forgive them ?

a_____

_____

b_____

_____

c_____

_____

LETTERS OF TRUTH, FORGIVENESS AND LOVE

Now write a letter (or a paragraph or more for each person) expressing what ever you feel that you need to communicate to them before departing from them.

You might like to express some needs, emotions, complaints, grievances, bitterness, feelings of injustice, disappointment, love, gratitude, secrets which you have held, what you admire in them or perhaps you would like to forgive the other or ask for forgiveness.

Try to be as honest and specific as you can.

You can write to each separately as you maintain the feeling that you are now about to be separated and will never again be in this specific relationship.

_____

_____

_____

_____

_____

_____

_____

_____

_____

_____

_____

_____

_____

_____

_____

_____

_____

_____

_____

_____

_____

_____

HOW WILL YOU COPE WITH THE
DEPARTURE OF YOUR LOVED ONES?

1. How do you imagine you will feel in the case of the departure of any of your close loved ones from their temporary physical bodies?

_____

_____

_____

_____

_____

_____

2. Do you feel fear concerning this possibility ? If yes, what do you fear the most concerning your loved ones' departure from their temporary physical bodies? Answer separately for each.

_____

_____

_____

_____

_____

_____

3.   Which truths or beliefs would you like to strengthen in order to be able to accept more peacefully the inevitable and totally natural fact that we are all temporary and that either you or your loved ones will be departing from your bodies before the other?

4.   What would you like to do or complete in relationship with your loved ones so as to be more ready for our or their depart from these temporary physical bodies.?

_____

_____

_____

_____

_____

COMFORTING BREATHING

**A method for comforting and bringing peace
and pain relief for dying persons.**

The subject lies on his or her back or takes any comfortable position
in which the lungs can be free.
The helper sits close enough to touch him or her during the process.
He guides the subject to breathe slowly and comfortably filling the
lungs as much as possible without exerting effort.

During the exhalation he shows the subject how to make the sound
"AAAAAAAAA" with his mouth slightly open, as if he is hissing,
or in some cases, moaning. All attention is on the breath as the
helper counts he number of breaths. If possible, the subject
imagines on the inhalation a light entering the body and leaving the
body on the exhalation. This is most effective if he or she *inhales
and exhales the light* at the part of the body which has pain.

AFTER, IF THE SUBJECT IS ABLE

1. He or she inhales into the soles of the **feet** bringing the energy
and/or *light* up to the hip joints and then on the exhalation out of
the soles of the **feet** again. (5 times)

2. He or she inhales the energy and/or light into the **solar plexus**
and then on the exhalation out of the soles of the **feet** again. (5
times)

3. He or she inhales the energy and/or light into the **solar plexus**
and then on the exhalation out of the **top of the head**. (5 times)

4. He or she inhales the energy and/or light into the **top of he
head** and then on the exhalation out of the soles of the **feet** again.
(5 times)

5. He or she inhales the energy and/or light into the bottom of the
feet and then on the exhalation out of the **top of the head**. (5
times)

6. He or she inhales the energy and/or light into the **forehead** and then on the exhalation out of the **top of the head**. (5 times)

7. He or she inhales and exhales in and out of the **top of the head**. (5 Times)

We can then guide him/her into a **deep relaxation** where he/she can imagine light flowing throughout the body and mind.

At any point we can **place our hands** on the various energy centers such as the solar plexus, the heart center in the center of the chest or the forehead or the top of the head. We can imagine energy, peace or light flowing through our hands into the other. We can also pray for the other.

May you be forever happy and in the Light

About Our Web Site www.HolisticHarmony.com

We have 30 years of experience in
helping people clarify and improve their lives

YOU MAY BE ABLE TO USE US TO:

1. Create **emotional harmony**
2. Improve your **health**
3. Develop inner **peace**
4. **Resolve** inner conflicts
5. **Communicate** more effectively and Harmoniously
6. Open your heart to **love**
7. **Accept** and love your self more
8. Develop **self confidence**
9. Cultivate **higher virtues**
10. Obtain greater **self-knowledge**
11. **Deal** with challenging tests
12. **Understand** what Life is asking you to learn
13. Develop your own **personal philosophy** of life
14. Clarify your **value system**
15. Make **decisions**
16. Strengthen the **truth** within
17. Increase your **creativity**
18. Become a **happier** person
19. **Overcome** fears
20. **Remove blockages** towards manifesting dreams
21. Improve your **meditation**
22. **Deal with death**, yours or loved ones
23. **Free** yourself from old emotional games
24. **Let go** of the past and future
25. **Accept your life** as it is
26. Develop your **relationship with the Divine**
And many others ways you might think of.

ABOUT THE AUTHOR

American born, Robert Elias Najemy is presently living in Athens Greece, were he has founded and is directing the **Center for Harmonious Living** since 1976 which serves 3500 members with classes and workshops designed to aid each in the improvement of his or her body, mind, relationships and life in general.

He has counselled and taught over 20,000 persons.

Robert has 20 books published in Greek, which have sold over 100,000 copies.

He is the author of hundreds of articles published in magazines in England, Australia, India and Greece.

He has developed a program of seminars for Self-Analysis, Self-Discovery, Self-Knowledge, Self-Improvement, Self-Transformation and Self-Realization. He has trained over 300 Life Coaches and does so now over the internet.

This system combines a wide variety of well-tested ancient and modern techniques and concepts

His teachings come from what he calls "Universal Philosophy" which is the basis of all religions and yet beyond and not limited by religions.

His seminars include a variety of experiences including:
1. Basic **psychological** and **philosophical teachings.**
2. Self analysis through specially designed questionnaires.
3. Methods of **contacting** and **releasing** the contents of the **subconscious** in a safe and gentle way.
4. Exercises, breathing, movement, **singing**, chanting and **dance** for expression and release.
5. Methods for **discovering and releasing** through **regressions** (in relaxation) the events of the past, which have programmed our minds negatively and thus, are obstructing our happiness and effectiveness in the present.
6. Techniques for **solving inner conflicts** and also for **solving conflicts with others**.
7. Methods for **calming the mind** and **creating positive mental states.**
8. Experiences for feeling greater unity with others and breaking through feelings of separateness.
9. Opportunities to **share with others** that which one is feeling and experiencing.
10. Emotional release techniques.
11. Methods of meditation and transcendence of the mind for those who are ready.

WHO ARE WE?

We are a group of life-management coaches working for the **CENTER OF HARMONIOUS LIVING** a non profit organization based for the last 25 years in Athens, Greece. We have aided over 20,000 people in clarifying their life issues through lectures, seminars, group work, books, cassettes, videos and personal appointments.

Benefit from our resources at
www.HolisticHarmony.com

1. Free Audio clips with Lectures and relaxation techniques:
http://www.HolisticHarmony.com/audioclips/index.asp

2. Books and ebooks at:
 http://www.HolisticHarmony.com/ebookscb/index.asp

3. Learn About Energy Psychology for free at:
http://www.HolisticHarmony.com/eft/index.asp

4. Become Trained as a Life Coach over the internet at:
http://www.HolisticHarmony.com/introholisticcoach.asp

5. Free Teleclasses and lectures as audio files:
http://www.HolisticHarmony.com/teleclasses/index.asp

6. Free email courses
http://www.HolisticHarmony.com/courses/index.asp

7. Free biweekly Ezine "Clarity"
To subscribe click: http://www.holisticharmony.com/register.asp

8. Free Articles on health, happiness, relationships etc.
http://www.HolisticHarmony.com/ezines/index.asp
With an Abundance of Information on

* Relationships	* Motivation & Positive Thinking
* Self-Acceptance	* Healing Our Inner Child
* Dealing With Emotions	* Health
* Contemporary Parables	* Death & Dying
* Meditation	* Spirituality
* Love	* Other Virtues

Books and ebooks
by Robert Elias Najemy

1. Universal Philosophy

2. The Art of Meditation

3. Contemporary Parables

4. The Mystical Circle of Life

5. Relationships of Conscious Love

6. The Miracles of Love and Wisdom

7. Free to be Happy with Energy Psychology by Tapping on Acupuncture Points

8. Saram – The Adventures of a Soul and Insight into the Male Psyche

9. The Psychology of Happiness

10. Petros Discovers the Truth

You can view them at:

www.HolisticHarmony.com/ebookscb.index.asp